IN OTHER WORDS, WEAR SHORTS

A YEAR ON CHRISTMAS ISLAND

Frank Craig was born in Bristol in 1936 and joined the R.A.F. at seventeen straight from Grammar School as an admin apprentice. He was posted to Christmas Island in August 1957, witnessing two of the biggest nuclear detonations in Operations Grapple X and Y. He left the R.A.F. in 1966 to become a geography teacher in Leeds. He took early retirement at sixty but soon returned, where he taught for fourteen years part-time "because I enjoy teaching so much." His passion is steam trains with photography thrown in.

IN OTHER WORDS, WEAR SHORTS

A YEAR ON CHRISTMAS ISLAND

FRANK CRAIG

All rights reserved. © Frank Craig 2008.

No part of this document may be reproduced, sold, stored in or introduced into a retrieval system, or transmitted, in any form or by any means (electronic, mechanical, photocopying, recording or otherwise), without the prior permission of the copyright owner.

First published 2008
This edition 2023

ISBN-13: 9798398570342

British Cataloguing Publication Data:
A catalogue record of this book is available from
The British Library.

For Dennis King, Alan Smith, Geoff Rogers, Paddy Kyle (Paddy and Geoff didn't make it) and all nuclear test veterans; especially those who still suffer or have not survived.

CONTENTS

- CONTENTS 6
- PROLOGUE 9
- INTRODUCTION 11
- **CHRISTMAS ISLAND** 13
  - GETTING THERE 15
  - THE ISLAND 19
  - BEACH AND REEF 22
- **MAIN CAMP** 31
  - THE TENTS AND D5 33
  - THE FOOD 44
  - N.A.A.F.I. 46
  - CAMP BARBERS 47
  - TO WORK 48
  - AT WORK 51
  - 24-HOUR GUARD 54
  - CHARACTERS 55
  - SEXUAL ORIENTATION 57
  - FREE CIGARETTES 58
  - THE ARMY ON CHRISTMAS 59
- **OFF-DUTY TIME** 61
  - THE LAGOONS 63
  - MUSIC CLUB 70
  - THE ASTRA 72
  - COVER-UP 74
  - COCONUTS HOME 77
  - PARTIES 78
  - WILDLIFE 82

THE GILBERTESE AND GRIMBLE	91
PERKS	97
POETRY!	122
No Wine Women or Song (Just Sand)	123
The Christmas Island National Anthem	127
La Reve Passe	129
Notice of Return	132
THE BOMB	**135**
HOMECOMING AND AFTER	**143**
GETTING BACK	145
HOMECOMING	152
ON REFLECTION	155
CONCLUSION	168
GLOSSARY	169

PROLOGUE

I can't rightly say what made me feel the sudden urge to bring back events from sixty years ago and want to set them down with the intention of recording what my Christmas Island exploits were. I had made a rough list of headings over forty years ago, meaning of course to follow it up while things were still clear in my memory, but did nothing more and eventually forgot where I'd put it. I was too busy bringing up a young family of five and starting out as a newly qualified teacher after my thirteen years R.A.F service ended, to embark on such a wordy, time-consuming project. It's only since joining the B.N.T.V.A. (British Nuclear Test Veterans Association) many years and a retirement later; meeting new friends – fellow "land crabs" – and becoming aware for the first time of the true scale of the whole health issue of nuclear veterans like me, that these refuelled my need to reassess the situation, put pen to paper and finger to keyboard. At the same time, I couldn't let these serious issues cloud those hilarious moments which, for me, there was certainly no shortage at the time.

A number of very readable books have already been written about this controversial period of our recent history, at all levels, from Task Force Commander, through bomber squadron leader to humble soldier and airman, so why add another to this impressive pile? In comparing my own mid-Pacific experiences with some of those already in print, I hope to show that many of the individual experiences there, as well as those major shared events, were personal to me, yet stimulating enough to be at least as readable as those others, some of which I will touch upon.

I found W.E. Oulton's "Christmas Island Cracker" macro view of the whole Grapple operation from the top, most fascinating, comprehensive and absorbing – a master lesson in organisational acumen and showing just what the old-boy network could achieve within such a tight, urgent, politically-driven schedule. But what of the micro-view – the everyday minutiae of island life endured during Operation Grapple – as seen by the lower-rank "erk" – tiniest cog in that massive nuclear wheel? I enjoyed reading J. Haggas' personal account: "Christmas Island – Wrong Place at the Wrong Time" albeit from the more closed Army environment of the artisan soldier's viewpoint, but nevertheless a stimulating, easy to identify with record of island life. Ken McGinley's book "No Risk Involved" on the other hand, left a nasty taste in my mouth from the outset. I found his harrowing, heroic story frankly heartbreaking, and can empathise with his marathon struggles for some kind of justice through the B.N.T.V.A. on behalf of the hundreds of servicemen and scientific civilians who left this period of nuclear testing history terribly scathed; successive governments' deliberate apathy and inaction gave me a sense of shame as our representative elected bodies.

I also felt very lucky not to be similarly affected myself, although I have become increasingly convinced that my daughter's leukaemia in 1984 was not entirely spontaneous, but a possible legacy of my year on Christmas Island. Neither were my wife's three earlier miscarriages.

Despite the obvious, shared Grapple experiences, one individual's story was inevitably different from another's, creating gaps in this coverage of events, which is where my story and related incidents hopefully fit in between – the ordinary airman-on-the-island's view.

Personally, I was fortunate enough to have enjoyed, overall, my year on this atoll, at least partly because I found much of interest to do and see in my off-duty time. These offset the rather primitive, much less salubrious conditions of routine daily life there that simply had to be tolerated with varying degrees of stoicism and success. Another factor was what I would call the "optimism of youth", in seizing any worthwhile opportunity that came my way – the island did have much to feed my curiosity and interests – adding to a memorable stay, whether looking on the positive or negative side.

INTRODUCTION

I can picture it now: 1957 – teenage years just left behind; a clerk in the R.A.F. on a twelve-year engagement, single and free, proud owner of my first motorbike, enjoying a life of athletics and new friends in a Salisbury Plain Command Headquarters – when I find myself on P.W.R. (Preliminary Warning Roll) for overseas service. I fill in the section on the form, asking me (!) for my three main choices in order of preference: where would I like to spend the next two or three years of my life? Optimistically as ever, I list: "Hong Kong, Ceylon (Sri Lanka) and Singapore". I can already see myself living it up in the Far Eastern sun. But this is 1957, the cold war nuclear arms race is bigger than my Far Eastern dreams, and I am brought down to earth with a hefty bump, with the news that a small, far-off atoll in the Mid-Pacific – ideal for letting off the odd megaton bomb – requires my services a little more urgently than, say, Hong Kong, Ceylon or Singapore. Oh well, maybe next time.

Meanwhile, back to reality, I learn that Christmas Island is a one-year unaccompanied tour to support a series of political tub-thumping British thermo-nuclear tests in the Pacific. The location sounds great, doesn't it – a mid-Pacific coral atoll – sun, sea, coral-sand, soft sea-breezes, blue lagoons, surf crashing softly over the reef and all the rest of it (even who knows, dusky maidens?). Fact, however, would turn out a little different than my wild imagination pictured it, but more of that later.

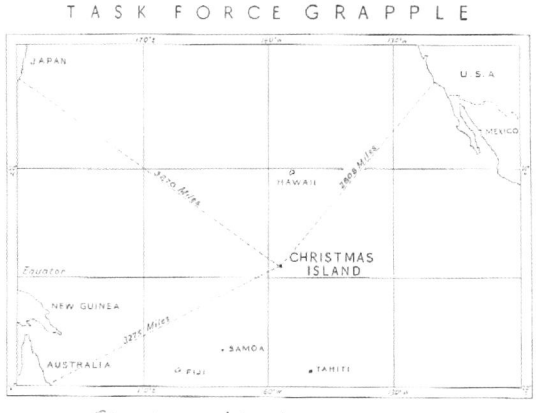

Christmas Island - This is where it is

CHRISTMAS ISLAND

GETTING THERE

Just one week after my twenty-first birthday I was packed off, along with an assortment of other R.A.F. unfortunates, to an isolated backwater of the Wiltshire countryside: Cliff Pypard R.A.F. Transit Camp, for flights to overseas parts, relieved of all my U.K. clothing – blues and civvies – and became proud owner of newly-issued tropical K.D. – rough, itchy, baggy, and fitting where it touched. There was still a day or so to go before our Comet flights from nearby R.A.F. Lyneham to points east, but for now we were confined to this transitory hill-top "cooler".

On our last evening of freedom, we discover there's an inviting village pub a mile or so down a winding country lane via the unofficial camp back entrance, but with nothing legal to wear. Latent travellers all, we had already made ad hoc friendship groups, having been thrown together over the last few hours: met on the train, on the shuttle bus to Cliff Pypard, allocated the same crowded transit billet or eating together crammed into the airmen's mess. So, around six of us newly assorted bodies locked heads to consider a solution to this novel problem – what to wear for our first and last camp breakout? Wandering rather aimlessly around camp we spotted a possible answer – scouts camping on a grassy slope conveniently near our hillside huts. Could this mean spare clothing maybe? I don't remember too clearly how willing or otherwise those young scouts were to part with their gear, but part with it they did. Scrambling straight into this odd assortment of apparel we made our jubilant way to the distant pub under a soft summer evening glow.

What a time we enjoyed at that welcoming bar on a late August evening: off to foreign parts next day, with or without hangovers, and living for the moment. Hours and many drinks later, in a purple haze, we somehow heaved ourselves out of the public bar at throwing out time, staggered back up the now pitch-dark leafy lane, loudly singing bawdy Service songs, more out of tune than in, hoping not to fall over each other too often and soil those kind scouts' assorted turnout – ill-fitting but perfect for the occasion. Eventually we found our way back to our billets in the warm summer darkness, hoping those generous young lads wouldn't need their gear back too soon. I think we even slept in them for what was left of the night, putting off changing into our itchy, ill-fitting K.D. as long as we could before being transported all too soon to Lyneham and the Comet fleet, bound by the eastward Pacific route to

Christmas Island and those nuclear tests.

We did manage one last escape to the local town, still clothed courtesy of those kindly scouts. The next afternoon saw a newly formed gang of ruffians (sorry, group of well-behaved airmen) let loose on an unsuspecting Swindon, limited only by the need to catch the last bus back to Cliff Pypard later that night. We swaggered noisily around town in those anonymous Scout cast-offs, chatting up the girls on our way, bragging of past exploits real and imagined, wondering what lay ahead over the next few months; bobbing into cafes for food and drink as required and generally enjoying the last of our short-lived freedom in U.K. Somehow the odd girl or two would join our happy band for a while, sometimes to disappear for a brief spell with one of our number, to reappear shortly after with a broad smile on his face, with or without new-found friend, with or without explanation. I wonder if that little timberyard is still there, door conveniently open? What it was to be young and long-gone tomorrow. Funnily enough, after the flight out, I never met up with any of these happy souls again on the island or thereafter, but the memories remain.

We should perhaps have been feeling the thrill of flying in these new Comet aircraft – maybe even a first flight for some of us. These were the very early days of long-haul jet air travel, but what little did we know or even care about those pioneering times – we had more immediate priorities and worries to occupy our young minds at the time. In any different context perhaps, this situation would have been brought home to us more pleasantly, but we were on our way to more urgent business – operational rather than leisure.

I don't remember too many details of our outward flight; our route and refuelling stops included I believe, Bahrain, in the Gulf; somewhere in India; Negombo (Sri Lanka) – it's all now a bit of a blur. It wasn't till we made our first Australian landfall at Darwin, Northern Territories, that we were given time to look around the local town. I recall Darwin in 1957 looking rather like an old timber-built wild west film set, complete with timber boardwalks, swing door saloon bars, dirt roads and sandy soil everywhere. Unfortunately, the local policemen, who looked more like U.S. sheriffs in their tan uniforms, weren't half as friendly or tolerant as our good old British Bobbies, so we were very careful how we spoke to them – and definitely no joking. At least the ex-pats welcomed us into their comfy bars. But, unknown to us at the time of course, things were about to change here; not long after, Darwin was to feel the full force of disastrous floods – their worst ever – which would inundate most of the town and would mean almost complete rebuilding.

Coincidentally, like the proverbial prophet of doom, I had visited Lynmouth before their disastrous floods, shortly before I joined the R.A.F. in the summer of 1953. Here, its normally peaceful stream was turned suddenly into a lethal torrent that uprooted the quiet, picturesque village, after continual, heavy rain inland had built up in the surrounding thin, sloping moorland soils above Lynmouth, becoming increasingly waterlogged until the accumulation suddenly burst down upon this North Devon village.

A Brisbane R.A.A.F. base, Amberley, was our next landfall, with no time even for a brief escape into town, although as it turned out, our evening escapade more than made up for that disappointment. It was Friday night – base airmen's dance night unknown to us when we arrived. The local Oz N.A.A.F.I. here, called Harry's Canteen, was the venue. Towards this spot we Poms gradually made our way, a few at a time, having spruced ourselves up as best we could after a long, sticky flight and still only our rumpled K.D. in which to strut our stuff. At first the local Aussie airmen greatly outnumbered us, so we early arrivals lurked warily on the sidelines keeping low profiles, but as more and more of we transients arrived, our numbers began to outweigh theirs. Wisely they gradually melted away into the night, helped on their way by our rousing crescendo of popular British patriotic songs – "There'll Always be an England" and "Rule Britannia" favourites to ensure their eventual departure. This left our raucous numbers to weigh up the local talent of the more tolerant and curious local Oz airwomen, with whom we danced and pranced the evening away until Cinderella hour – transit lights-out bedtime. What an evening we had enjoyed – well-stocked bar, dancing partners, willing and unwilling, an important moral victory over our antipodean oppos, and Pacific-bound in a few hours' time.

Next day we were off again, but not before civil Qantas Super-Constellation airliners were hastily requisitioned to replace our ailing, overworked and now unserviceable R.A.F. Comets, to transport us, by now in our hundreds, the rest of the way to Christmas Island, via Fiji. Breakfast on Fiji the following morning, as I recall, was served by male waiters, resplendent in dazzling white Cinderella serrated skirts and Village People hairdos. Then off up again, and almost before we realised, we had reached our destination, two-thirds of the way round the world: that low-slung, ocean-hugging, pure-white, sun-baked coral atoll 'paradise', shaped like a gigantic open-ended spanner, was to be our nuclear 'home' for the next year.

The moment we landed and stepped out of our comfortable Oz airliner, the heat and sun hit us. Herded unceremoniously on to a fleet of rut-weary three-ton Bedford trucks, suspensions "shot", we bumped and rattled our way to the Main Camp several uncomfortable miles away, along a road that despite its endless corrugations, we would, over the next few months daily journeys to work, come to know intimately, and would just have to get used to. Our accommodation for the duration turned out to be rows of rather small, tatty tents, with countless guy-ropes to trip over at night and stifling inside until we became acclimatised, with some light relief when their valances were rolled up for improved ventilation and for what limited cooling breezes decided to blow each day.

Tent D5

We would come to appreciate many of life's little comforts that we'd simply taken for granted in the UK., that here would be in rather short supply or even non-existent – until we returned home again in a year or so later.

THE ISLAND

To give some idea of the island's climate and weather, its Equatorial Dry Zone climate provides a fairly even temperature – around 80 deg. F (27 deg. C) throughout the year with frequent but irregular rainfall, but no separate rainy season. Tropical temperatures are mollified by its oceanic position. Easterly sea breezes blow throughout the year, but tropical storms – blame the Inter-Tropical Front – aren't unknown.

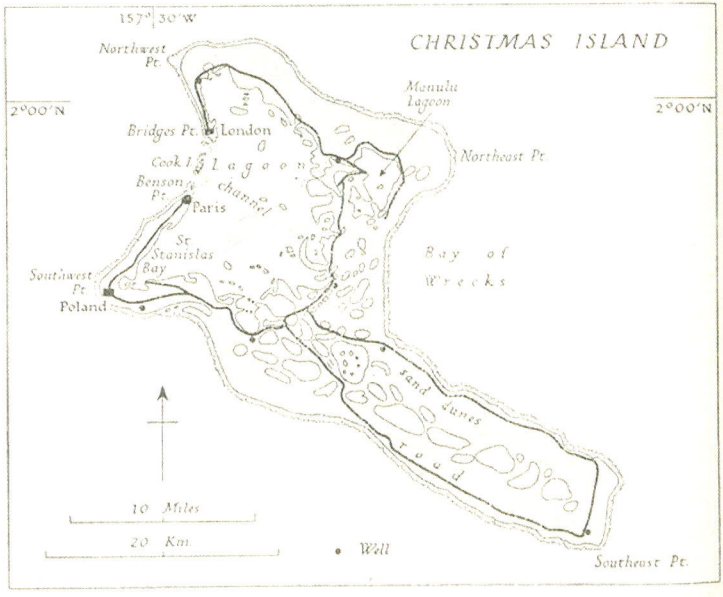

Fig. 146. Christmas
For general key to symbols see p. 8. Based on: (1) U.S.H.O. chart no. 1839; (2) Admiralty chart no. 2867; (3) K. P. Emory, *Bernice P. Bishop Museum Bulletin*, no. 123, p. 18 (Honolulu, 1934).

Christmas Island map

The island is a coral atoll – the world's largest at nearly 30 miles long – and rises little above sea level, almost nowhere above about 10 feet high. The tidal range is small, but the wide fringing coral reef goes from sea level to two thousand fathoms plus in just a short distance offshore, enough to produce dangerous backwash currents especially at high tide. These are strong enough to sweep the unwary bather out to and maybe over, the hard, jagged reef, from which few would return, even though the water is only up to three feet deep at high tide on the reef's landward side.

The lagoon

The continual muffled booming of the breakers pounding against the reef – most romantic in happier circumstances – form a ceaseless backdrop throughout day and night. The rain, although irregular, can be very heavy, but tends to fall in relatively short bursts and could quickly lead to localised flooding depending on the exact lie of the generally flat land.

Breakers over the waves

After a particularly heavy downpour, parts of our tented main camp would end up under water, forcing the unfortunate occupants to move elsewhere until re-accommodated. Although the compacted coral sand is not very absorbent, the rainfall soon dries up and disappears with the heat and rapid evaporation, when some kind of normality would gradually return.

Most of us were accommodated, crowded together at Main Camp in that assorted array of refugee tents, with rows of taps and metal washbasins at each end, with showers located just around the corner, but unfortunately too close to the toilets. Each day we would all disperse our separate ways to work after breakfast – to the Airfield Site, Port London, various stores, messes, offices, sick quarters, sewage farm(!) and many other workplaces, in and out of doors that were dotted around the north-west side of the island.

Sunrise on Christmas Island

BEACH AND REEF

The beach that fringed the island was of almost pure white coral sand. It was gently sloping and not very wide – up to about forty yards – merging almost imperceptibly with the low-lying land of the atoll, where stunted green scrub began. The tidal range was small. This was of course the favourite area for sunbathing, relaxing, drinking, paddling and studying the myriad tropical fish that abounded in the clear shallow water between reef and beach, a welcome change from stifling, overcrowded tents.

Beach scene

The reef was almost invisible from the beach, apart from its bumpy, harmless-looking tops exposed at low tide. A much better view of the reef's extent and shape could be had from the air, flying in or out of the island in the aircraft that took people and freight to and from Hawaii and other islands. From this viewpoint, the long, deadly corrugations of the reef's deep green fingers could be clearly seen on the seaward side, disappearing darkly to great depths – thousands of fathoms to the Pacific floor; the breakers constantly foamed white to landward. Like Scylla and Charybdis of Greek legend, it was fatal to be caught in its jagged embrace between inner and outer margins, yet beautiful to look at from above or simply to close your eyes and listen to from the safety of the beach.

View of the reef at low tide

We could sometimes make out a common sight in the landward shallows of the reef - shoals of bonefish, at about a metre long, their fins and tails often breaking the surface as the tide flowed and ebbed; apparently feeding on something tasty enough to attract them into these shallows by their activity. They were visible enough from the beach to be able to take a reasonably clear photograph of them.

Sunday morning relaxation

Early morning on the beach

Although considered by many to be an eyesore off the beautiful white beach opposite Main Camp, an aged pile of rusting vehicle wrecks, left years ago by vacating American forces during the Second World War, was a source of fascination for many of us – inviting a cautious wade in at low tide for tentative exploration, with their air of rusty abandonment, but yet photogenic in their corroded clutter.

M.T. wrecks off beach

They also posed questions for the more curious: who once drove these vehicles; in what circumstances; were they driven, dragged or towed down the beach as far as possible and simply left there, or were they craned out?

American wrecked M.T

Not worth repairing on the spot, or the cost of transporting them on to the next theatre of operation, of no further use to the occupying forces about to leave the island for good, they rested where they were dumped, gathering rust and coral, providing convenient hiding places for the innumerable tropical fish that played and hid within.

Breakers and old wrecks

A roped-off safety area was established at a central area of the main camp beach, and a lifeguard tower, manned by a "duty corporal", built to supervise the bathers. Paddling was a safer way of relaxing here, as the water was only about knee-deep – not deep enough to swim, which would have been a more dangerous activity, as loss of contact with the bottom could render the swimmer prone to sudden strong backwash currents and the possibility of being swept out over the reef and oblivion.

Spear fishing

A little more risky, especially outside the safety area, was nevertheless a favourite pastime of snorkelling off the beach, with diving mask and maybe flippers. At incoming high tide, you held your head underwater and watched the tiny multi-coloured tropical fish darting in and out of the coral on the landward side of the reef, swimming to and fro in front of you, with the tide's ebb and flow. Because of the strong backwash of each wave, it was vital at these moments to keep a firm grip on any projecting coral to prevent the possibility of being swept out towards the reef, if it was not shallow enough to be able to stand or crawl safely on the bottom. Even at a depth of only two feet, the backwash could sweep you out if you were in an unattached horizontal position, so a firm grip was always vital, and of course you should remain inside the roped-off safety area, within sight of the duty corporal lifeguard. I remember when I was Duty Corporal on lifeguard stint one day, an octopus had been caught and landed somehow, then spread-eagled like a grisly cartwheel, embarrassingly for the unfortunate octopus, on one of the round coffee tables that littered the beach immediately below my perch atop the look-out tower. Although no giant by any stretch of the imagination, it was still about four or five feet between tentacle tips. I was reminded of a similar incident, but with the octopus captured in its own element below the waves, vividly described in Arthur Grimble's book about his stay with the Gilbertese Islanders (A Pattern of Islands) in the early nineteen-hundreds.

With the octopus

Sunbathing was of course the most popular form of relaxation on the beach, at almost any daylight hour. There were so many gorgeous stretches of handy beach that it never became overcrowded with the browning bodies of sun-worshippers, although for some unaccountable reason the proximity to the N.A.A.F.I. and its well-stocked bar during opening hours, meant that for the lazier inmates who didn't see the need to move more from sunbathing to re-stocking of liquid refreshment, resulted in this area being slightly more congested than usual at this time of day or evening. The range of body-tanning shades was extensive, as I mention later.

Frank Craig hunting a pufferfish

For serious drinkers, especially those bent on making the most of an organised party alfresco, the beach again was a popular choice of venue. The island, because of its tropical latitude throughout the year, would suddenly darken into evening sunset in a few brief moments just before seven pm, providing a certain anonymity to groups of revellers – also a good spot for novices to learn the more popular service songs that often floated on the evening air at party time, particularly as lubrication levels and camaraderie increased with ale intake. I don't remember how the mountains of beer-can litter were cleared up the following day – probably one of the less popular duties of the S.W.O. and his gang of admin orderly slaves.

Beach looking towards the Guard Tower

The beach would assume a greater beauty at sunrise and sunset, when the rising or setting sun reflected on sea and sand each in their different ways, often to wonderful effect. Had our situation on the island been different, the term "romantic" could certainly have sprung to mind. Unfortunately, the Cold War and nuclear ambitions of the West utterly cancelled out any chance of such a sentimental atmosphere, but they could still be spectacular at times.

Frank Craig posing for Mr Puniverse (searching for a skyhook)

MAIN CAMP

THE TENTS AND D5

The tents on our Main Camp lines were in varying states of dilapidation – usually manned with six to a tent, and sporting only very basic furniture – bedside lockers and camp beds only inches from the floor, with coconut matting down, hence prone to the occasional nocturnal visit from rats and land-crabs. Electricity cables were slung from tent to tent, to power a single light bulb in each. We did experience the occasional spectacular electrical storm at night – continuous on-off-on-off sheet lightning – silent and eerie; rarely but frighteningly, also ball lightning that somehow seemed to me to travel along the power cables. Tents could easily catch fire and occasionally did burn down, usually by a careless smoker. When this did happen very little remained afterwards – a black patch in the sand, with smouldering lockers and personal effects. Life inside our tents was obviously cramped, so we all had to learn to live equably with each other, in such close proximity; a sense of humour played an important part here. All tents were numbered – ours was D5.

Relaxing off-duty outside the tent

During the day we usually rolled up the tent sides to improve ventilation and lower the humid temperature inside as much as we could, hoping a strong wind wouldn't suddenly gust and create a minor dust-storm to cover our precious belongings and beds with fine coral sand. Having some idea of dominant wind direction (invariably from the east) helped, so we could hopefully leave one or two tent sides down for at least some protection.

Wind and sand were impartial – if they blew on one tent, they blew on them all. We coped somehow. I don't remember if S.N.C.O.s and officers were similarly accommodated and protected, but I imagine they would have had their share of what we had to put up with.

Some must have been green-fingered, judging by the occasional array of sprouting coconut plants in neatly raked sand, often bounded by ordered, regimented squares of white coral-block stones; these were usually imposed by the Army hierarchy as "good for discipline, chaps".

Some of our mobile homes sported rather pretentious nameplates at their front entrances. I liked these – most were cleverly original. Two that I particularly remember and still have a chuckle over, were "Hugget and Bucket Haulage Contractors" and "Furkham Hall"; there must have been others equally good, but I've forgotten them. To keep up with the Joneses, one day I made one for D5 – "Louse House"- in rather snappy red and silver painted on wood, in memory of a tent companion's temporary lodgers at one stage. I was quite proud of that. Not to be outdone, the next tent, D4, promptly followed suit, with a rough and ready, black-painted post with "The Backbone – A.V.M. Oulton" daubed in yellow – a reference to words of praise made by our Task Force Commander, to the airmen on the island, for their efforts under such difficult conditions.

Sharing life's little discomforts in D5 were six of us: Pete from Birmingham, Joe from Yorkshire, Derek from London, Geordie Dennis, Geoff from Manchester, and myself from Gloucestershire – a right regional and cultural mix! We got on well with each other – we had to – and became firm and loyal friends, sharing many of our duty, off-duty and mealtimes, as well as life's little trials, together. Our varied personalities did gel to form a tight little D5 community – if we hadn't, life would have been much less bearable.

New Year's party in Tent D5

Dennis was a D5 inmate who became a close friend – one of the few I have kept in touch with ever since. A canny Northumbrian, I eventually came to understand his Geordie accent, especially after he taught me their national song "Sweet Cushie Butterfield" – then I could almost speak like him! At one uncomfortable period for him, he was afflicted by a number of additional sleeping companions, and after a spell of wondering why his skin was so itchy in the morning, the solution was soon supplied to him by a friend from a nearby tent who had suffered the same problem a short while before. He searched Dennis' bed and promptly discovered an infection of bloated bedbugs, an aspect of the island's wildlife I almost forgot to mention. The friend recommended what had worked for him – a mixture of paraffin and water liberally applied to all parts of his bed, especially their favourite hiding place, the seams. Dennis wisely chose the lesser of the two evils by lying at night on a rank-smelling, paraffin-soaked bed, rather than having to be eaten alive by bedbugs; eventually it worked, and our tent gradually lost that pervasive, slightly stifling smell. Dennis was always good fun to be with – that did help in our situation there.

Pete Harrison's 21s¹ birthday party at the NAAFI

Pete was a self-assured Brummie; he was an excellent swimmer and played water polo for Birmingham. Mysteriously he always seemed to turn up in my photographs somehow, usually in beach scenes, at daybreak or early dusk, striking a suitable pose.

One day at the lagoons he was to put his swimming ability to the test, saving Dennis' life when he got into difficulties trying to rescue a drowning non-swimmer. Dennis had noticed that this person had managed with some difficulty to reach the diving raft where he and Pete were playing, climbed on, but somehow over-balanced and fell off again, into relatively deep water. Unable to swim well and no doubt with a mouthful of very salty water, he started to drown.

Dennis spotted him, jumped in to save him, managing to grab him by a leg. The casualty in panic gripped Dennis' leg and would not let go, pulling him under. Although Dennis had managed to take a good deep breath before being dragged under, he himself was now in trouble from the drowning man's clutches; Pete saw what was happening, dived in and managed to loosen the man's grip on Dennis, bringing them both back on to the raft and safety. Dennis has never forgotten this incident or his gratitude to Pete.

New Year' party in Tent D5

Another of our tent "characters" was Joe from South Yorkshire. He was an Admin. Orderly, one of the S.W.O.'s personal "slaves" employed mainly in unloading ships at Port London and generally clearing up around camp. Occasionally things would "fall off a lorry" and he would return to our tent with a bulging K.D. shirt. One day we were all treated to tins of "Roses" talc, replete with strong but tasteful bouquet – for women. Later that day we all made our way to the showers, redolent with Roses – to face a reaction of catcalls and derision from the showers' other occupants. We quickly and quietly disposed of our new acquisitions as soon as Joe wasn't around – he didn't seem too upset afterwards: we hoped he didn't notice. Another time he came back, shirt stuffed with chocolate bars. You can guess what state they were in – what with the ambient temperature and humidity, added to Joe's own body heat and sweat. We were grateful for the chocolate but spent most of the next few days painfully separating knots of foil wrapper from sadly misshapen blobs of chocolate bar. Never again. At one time there were not one, but two jerry-cans in our tent: one of the usual drinking water, the other – hopefully a temporary measure – a mixture of paraffin and water to help Dennis get rid of his new sleeping companions. Joe's tin mug wasn't what you would call the cleanest in the tent.

Dennis and Dave

One day when we returned from work (he either seemed always to be back before us, no matter how far he'd been that day, or he'd disappear for days on end on same far-flung job or other for the S.W.O,.) he was drinking from his mug with an odd expression on his face, muttering that his water tasted "a bit funny". Dennis quickly sniffed his mug, turned up his nose and put him right – Joe had mistakenly filled his mug from Dennis' paraffin-mix jerry-can. Joe lamely replied that he thought it was because his mug "needed washing". That was Joe – ever the mystified optimist.

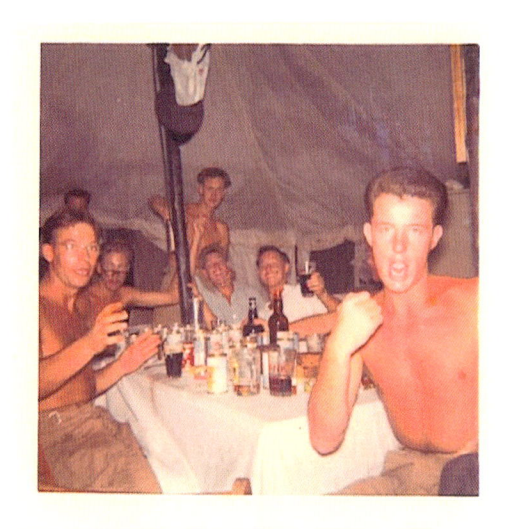

New Year's party in Tent D5

Another of our tent occupants was Derek, a Londoner with a crew-cut, powerfully built, I remember, but very affable, easy-going and with another quality that wasn't always advisable in our circumstances – unsuspecting trust. Our drinking water came in the form of a five-gallon jerry-can which, because of our constant thirsts, had to be refilled daily. When full, the jerry-can tended of course to be rather heavy, so not everyone was always willing to make the effort taking their turn filling it at the taps at the end of our tent lines and lugging it back. We tried various ways of taking turns – making rotas, which weren't always strictly followed; allocating a day per occupant, again rather open to rather loose interpretation; drawing lots via names out of a hat – a bit hit-and-miss for some, especially, as it turned out, in one short period, for the trusting Derek. For this third method, it fell to the ever-canny Dennis to take "responsibility" for writing each name on a piece of paper, folding each piece religiously and putting them into the "hat". Unknown to us at first, he wrote Derek's name on every piece of paper, which of course resulted in Derek's name being drawn out for the water run each time – perhaps three or four times, until it became too risky to push our luck further, even for the unsuspecting Derek. Meanwhile, Derek had been scratching his head with puzzlement, wondering why his name seemed to come up so regularly. Fortunately, he never did twig while Dennis pushed his luck with the "hat" method.

Pete Harrison's 21st birthday party

Geoff completed our tent complement – a quiet lad with a dry sense of Lancastrian humour, with Cheshire overtones. He was greatly missing his girl-friend Eileen and wrote to her most days, marrying her on his return. I went to see him at Newton Hyde long after we returned, as a surprise guest at his 50th birthday celebration. I mention him again, under the unlikely heading of "Wildlife".

Dennis King, Pete, Derrick and Pete

An odd mixture of general gossip would filter down the immediate tent grapevine from time to time, to be ingested, sampled and spat out again maybe if the trivia failed to excite sufficient interest; if it did pass the acid test, it would be followed up and made something of, usually in order to take our minds off our own occasional Christmas blues. One such item that did get straight through was so original and daring that it made us get up off our beds and join in with the spirit of the thing. Such were the conditions on the island that a variety of ploys were tried by some individuals attempting to "work their ticket" back to U.K. prematurely. One such effort by an acquaintance in a nearby tent to affect a psychological disorder caught our imaginations so well that we just had to join in with the charade. This person decided he "owned" an invisible horse and to his credit he kept up the act for quite a while, and to the extent that he searched daily for (and presumably found?) suitable sustenance for it, leaving it outside his tent where the beast was stabled. We joined in with a will, as much for the novelty value as for the neighbourly gesture and would help him search for the necessary equine nourishment. He even went so far as to build a proper hitching rail outside his tent. Unfortunately, he ended up completing his full stint on the island like the rest of us; what happened to his faithful four-legged friend (I think it was called Trigger) when he left, I can only imagine. As I have said, this did tend to show the lengths to which some people would go to affect a premature end to their time on the island, and I for one couldn't blame them for most of the time.

More than one airman I knew grew increasingly stressed as their island life dragged, especially as repatriation approached, near the end of their year's stay. Home was beginning to be so near yet so far away, and time did seem to crawl as thoughts turned to that magical day when the island would at last disappear into the vast Pacific Ocean as you flew away from the unfortunate atoll, homeward at last. Meanwhile your daily routine had to be grudgingly followed, and any little incident that disturbed this tunnel-vision of dogged concentration – good or bad – could produce a sudden, even violent reaction. This was the case one day, shortly before our group of friends with about the same time to go before repatriation, were due for return. Eddie, named after a famous trumpeter namesake, was certainly one such stressed individual. He could be seen ominously simmering away more and more often. My Geordie friend Dennis, who was also due to leave the island, had to do an extra off-duty job for one of the Headquarters officers, and had asked, half-jokingly, if his name could be added to the flight list for the next plane home. When the officer agreed, telling him to add his name to the list, he pushed his luck further and asked if his friend Eddie's name could also be added, to which the officer again agreed; so it was official that both would be flying home within days. Dennis, elated, made a point of telling Eddie the good news as soon as he next saw him, back at the tents. Eddie must have been in one of his stressful moods because, as soon as Dennis broke the news to him, his first reaction was to explode: he punched Dennis on the chin! Obviously, he didn't believe what he had been told, expecting a trick was being played, raising his hopes only to have them dashed when the joke unfolded. Dennis took this in good part, and Eddie apologised as soon as he saw his name confirmed on the embarkation list. But it just went to show the different ways that life on the island could wear you down and produce spontaneous adverse reactions that could have had unfortunate results. There must have been many such incidents it's just that we simply couldn't get to know more than a few, which happened within our immediate surroundings.

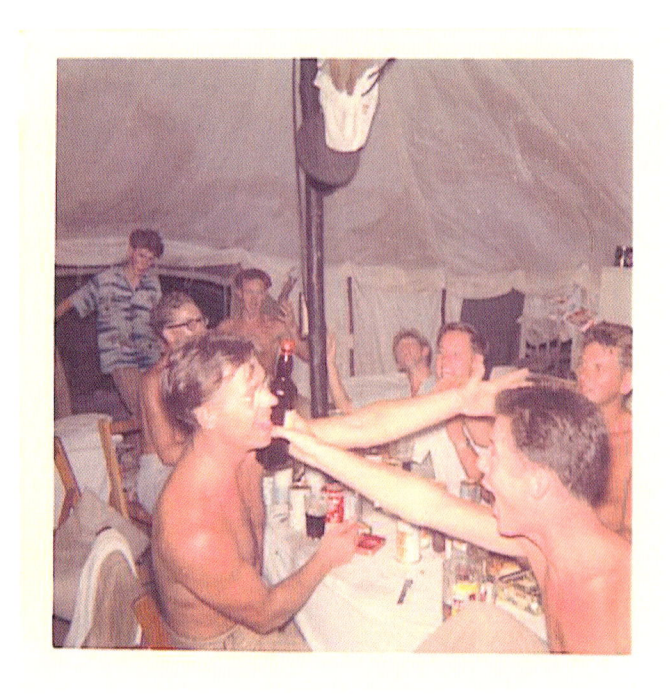

New Year's party in Tent D5

It was a fact of tent life that certain fads that did the rounds caught on more widely than others. Such was the case at one period, with moustaches. Their cultivation among us caught on rather well. Not to be outdone by the promising growths on my friends' upper lips, I decided to have a go myself. I stopped shaving this part of my face for a few weeks, waiting for it to assume the luxuriant proportions of my colleagues', but with no obvious result. Disappointed, deflated and a bit ashamed, I shaved off the sparse growth, but not before I had taken a photograph of my failed attempt, just for the record. Once was enough; I've never tried it since.

For most of our stay on the island we each wrote more or less regularly to female penfriends in the U.K., found for us by one of our number – the first to write home and receive a reply. He then asked if his new penfriend had any mates who would write to the others in the tent; so it spread to the rest of us who were unspoken for, and these regular letters to and from "back home", nicely occupied some of our spare time. I remember that, in the end, mine, a girl from Manchester called Barbara, was the only one in our tent to keep up the correspondence for the whole of our time on the island, the others having lost interest and dried up at one point or another. Because of this, I arranged to meet her on my return to U.K., during my disembarkation leave; I screwed up my courage, jumped on my motorbike, rode up to Manchester and met Barbara at a corner café near her home. My suggestion of a holiday together on my bike tempted her, but was later that day, on second thoughts, turned down. I rode back home sadder and not much wiser, and never met again! However, our period of mail exchange on the island had filled a small but useful niche.

With best wishes for a very Happy Christmas

THE FOOD

The food, for want of a better word, every single meal of my stay on the island – with the exception of just one better but less than brilliant Christmas dinner – could sometimes be barely edible. I suppose the Army cooks did their best with what they were supplied with – all "fresh" food was flown in courtesy of 1325 Flight Dakota air taxi service ("Christmas Airways") thrice-weekly long-haul flights from Hawaii, almost 1500 miles away: nothing could be grown in our island's coral sand. The worst item, which still turns my stomach at the thought of it, was "pom" – dehydrated powdered potato, which oozed glutinously and tastelessly over our tin trays, unwilling to leave them by knife, fork or spoon. Ugh!

As I have mentioned, the culinary high spot of our year was the Christmas lunch. The menu may look impressive on the creased and wrinkled copy I still have, but in reality, it didn't give that meal its true seasonal quality. I must admit it was better than the rest of what passed for food on the island, but it was inevitably still far below what we would have dined on at home in any airmen's mess in the U.K., so we enjoyed the brief improvement while it lasted. For us though, the main attraction that day was the ice-cream course, by far the most sought-after part of the meal, and the only time I remember having this treat on the island. There was the consequently long queue, but for us, well worth waiting in line for. Some of us, however, felt morally driven to cheat a little by joining the queue a second time; having wolfed down our first sitting in record time, we surreptitiously re-joined the end of the queue, quietly threw away our second first course and grabbed a second slab of ice-cream, with lowered eyes that wouldn't meet the eagle-eyed gaze of the cooks who of course guessed that this would happen. But it tasted better I'm sure, for the way it was obtained.

Our divided tin trays were theoretically supposed to separate courses – potato from pudding, gravy from custard. The mess cooks seemed determined to achieve the opposite in their desire for speedy completion of our meals, which were strictly timed, so that they could clear away and begin again to plan what culinary delight to spoil for tomorrow's offering. Because what they did dole out to us was often pretty unpalatable, this helped process us through more rapidly anyway.

As if food quality wasn't quite up to Cordon Bleu standards, there were also, always lying in wait for us on the tables, in uninviting white piles, salt tablets to replace that lost in our daily sweat, of which we shed buckets. Although an indispensable part of our diet, like all best medicines seemingly, they tasted awful. I'd swear sometimes that these were put out for the cooks to get their own back for our unfavourable comments as we filed past the servery: the looks on their faces would say, in true doctor- patient fashion, "This'll hurt us more than it will you." However, stop taking them and your health wouldn't last long out there – you could die so easily from salt-deficiency. So, before leaving the mess, we'd either put a brave face on it, take our punishment like men, and force a tablet down with a resigned sigh and appropriate agonised expression (so the cooks would notice and feel pleased), or else furtively take one to eat later in private, so as not to put a public face on our private pain of distaste when swallowing that bitter pill.

Meals finished, we washed our trays and eating irons at the communal taps at one end of the tent lines, where we found the most effective grease remover was coral sand – and that, you could say, was in plentiful supply in this part of the world.

Another problem, associated with food, was the strategic weakness of our communal showers' position between tents and toilets and the frequency with which we could become temporarily afflicted with what we called "the screamers" – a mild form of dysentery, which would affect us all sooner or later, some more frequently and severely than others. This necessitated the rapid departure from your tent (or wherever you happened to be at the time you felt the urgent need) to the nearest toilet. If your bout was serious, there wasn't always time to make the full distance, which was one important reason, especially during the hours of darkness, with almost complete lack of artificial lighting, for you to inspect the shower floor before using it. I occasionally heard, from within Tent D5, a distinct howl of anguish, followed by quite strong language, coming from the direction of the showers, by someone less than cautious and sharp-eyed. It was an unfortunate situation, but yet another feature of main camp life that you occasionally had to allow for.

N.A.A.F.I.

The N.A.A.F.I. shop when it opened, made a smart new improvement to our spending abilities – its range of goods on sale excellent compared with the previous W.V.S. place. Most important, you could buy a good selection of canned beer, but as yet, I don't think that can-lining technology had caught up with the acidic qualities of cider – my favourite west-country tipple. There were other, less common items like shark-fishing hooks and other esoteric articles. The manager- Jock – became as much a fixture as his shop and would always do his best to stock things you couldn't find at the time. Cigarettes, at duty-free prices, seemed so cheap to me – a non-smoker – that they sold in round tins of fifties rather than the usual tens or twenties. The empty tins could always be made use of after, if only as ad hoc ash trays. The N.A.A.F.I. opened out on to the beach at the front – a conveniently short journey for a drinking bout to begin; with an enclosed compound at the rear, for more private functions.

Jock – NAAFI Shop proprietor

CAMP BARBERS

There were at least two camp barbers when I was there – a jolly Cockney and a tall, thin Welshman. I became friendly with Allan the Londoner when we discovered a mutual passion for motorbikes. He liked trials riding while I just liked being mobile – at that time being able to get from A to B (mostly R.A.F. camp to home) and back. Allan had motorcycling magazines sent out regularly from the U.K., which became so popular with the local motorcycling fraternity they were lovingly passed round many times. Their condition occasionally became a little more tatty, beyond the normal "fair wear and tear" when the glue of their bindings was eaten by the local rats supplementing their diets with this chance delicacy if left lying around.

We returned home more or less at the same time and arranged to meet again on holiday at the Isle of Man T.T. Races the following June, where among other things we drove at great speed around the famous circuit – the wrong way – on the aptly-named "Mad Sunday" before the races proper began. We were accommodated at a farmhouse in Onchan, right next door to where the Japanese team Honda – there for their very first T.T. competition, pretty well swept the board with their superior machines – precision-built like watches – and the first time the world had seen square headlights. Looking at a photograph of myself on rocks above the beach at Douglas also made me realise how much weight I'd put on in the eleven months since I'd left the island – all my mother's fault really, for considering that her son was seriously undernourished on his return and feeding me up worse than a Christmas turkey. Allan and I have kept in touch ever since.

TO WORK

My daily work routine began as always with an unwillingness to wake up and get going. Our washing facilities – basic if not quite primitive – were "the taps" at the end of our tent lines. There was never any running hot water – or cold – always tepid – ambient temperature stuff. I think it was diluted seawater, with only that awful salt-water soap to wash with, which would never lather properly. After, hunger drove us towards the mess – full of unkept promises of better food to come. The humidity and heat were already doing their best to enervate us and make us unwilling to go to work.

Old S.H.Q

Along with most of my immediate friends, I worked as a secretarial clerk at S.H.Q. (Station Headquarters), located at the distant Airfield Site, before they built us a shining, new silver one right next to our main camp tent lines, halfway through my stay.

Our daily trek to the Airfield Site was by a small fleet of three-ton Bedford lorries with wooden slat seats, not quite A1 Taxi Service standards, but all there were. They had all seen better days, with suspensions well and truly "shot" by the countless potholes and ruts on the compacted coral-dust road that led to work. This furrowed desert highway was also liberally littered with dead, dying or simply confused land crabs, that scuttled, sometimes more, but often less successfully out of our way as best they could while crossing the road, like so many side-stepping Christmas Island crustacean chickens.

New S.H.Q

We soon became used to the regular squishy "plop" of the unlucky ones that prematurely met their end under the lorries' wheels, and, who knows, went to meet their maker in that great crab-paradise in the sky, where no doubt they were issued with suitable haloes from heavenly stores, to spend the rest of their sainted lives looking down to earth, endlessly checking up on their innumerable cousins as they in their turn crossed our hazardous highways, playing that risky game of roadside roulette to decide which of their number would duly join their brothers and sisters in the sky

Those of us who occasionally let their vivid imaginations run amok in this daily journey, did so, I swear, as some kind of momentary escape from the slow, punishing, backside-numbing ride on those slatted Bedford benches and countless holes in the road. These potholes, innocuously filled with pools of still water after frequent heavy rain, would, if you are gullible enough to believe me, swallow three-ton lorries and their contents whole, never to be seen again. Our M.T. drivers seemed to hold one of two opposing views on how to negotiate these craters and ridges: either that the faster they drove, the less their long-suffering passengers would feel them; or they would drive dead slow, constantly twisting to avoid the unavoidable (holes and land-crabs), invariably arriving late at our destination. How most of us avoided both acute and chronic travel-sickness and bruised behinds, I'll never know.

If you were lucky enough (I never was), a rare treat of a ride to or from work at the Airfield Site, was on the back of a Queen Mary – a long, flat-bed lorry with raised, trellised sides, used for transporting aircraft and their parts. Their suspensions were more softly sprung and gave a much more comfortable ride than a Bedford truck along those rutted roads. You would stand on the platform, hold on to the sides, and be conveyed by a transport of comparative delight.

By the lagoon gathering coconuts

AT WORK

My job was clerical – a 'chairborne' airman – typing and reproducing orders, letters, mail, filing and all the other office jobs that made our officers' lives even easier. Our immediate bosses were the Senior N.C.O. clerks and the adjutant (the boss's right-hand man), who were responsible to the various administrative officers in Headquarters, who in their turn were responsible to the C.O. – Group Captain Station Commander; he ultimately carried the can for all the island's servicemen. One of my jobs was typing and distributing S.R.O.s (Station Routine Orders), handed to me weekly by the adj., and after checking my work, for onward distribution. One amusing incident concerned a minor typing error I once made, not picked up by the adj., and sent out complete with mistake, much to the merriment of certain esoteric technical types who well understood the error. I had to type a warning about the presence of an old fuel dump which could be hazardous if you approached too near, due to the emission of potentially dangerous fumes which were rather volatile. In my hurry to complete the orders I mistyped the word "versatile" for "volatile" – a great source of amusement to the cognoscenti. Later I heard how hilarious some found my version; I hoped I remained anonymous at the time.

One of the facts of airfield H.Q. life was the liability of the whole area to regular flooding – that monsoon-type rain again – not enough to stop us working, but enough to be a nuisance when moving around the affected area.

Flooded tents

They say every cloud has a silver lining: some of the admin orderly runners (messengers) would enjoy taking advantage, using the shallow water as a chance to practise and show off new-found water-sport skills by aquaplaning through the floods on their bikes, or to have a quick "accidental" paddle in order to cool off in the heat of the day – even when cloudy the relative humidity was high enough to be very uncomfortable. However, much rain had accumulated, we just had to wait for the heat and rapid evaporation to do their bit in what came naturally.

C.O. inspecting the floods

Another useful diversion presented itself one day at the airfield site. A "sniffer" Canberra aircraft returned one day from a practice sortie with undercarriage problems: one main wheel would not lower for landing, so the pilot tried an assortment of ad hoc manoeuvres to try and dislodge the faulty wheel, but to no avail. We at airfield H.Q. soon found out what was happening through the local grapevine, so we all rushed out to see what would happen: we weren't disappointed. It came in as slowly as the sweating pilot dared without stalling his Canberra and dropping out of the sky; touched down on one wheel and ran the length of the runway quite evenly until inertia took over and it tilted sideways, coming to a sedate halt with minimum damage; a difficult landing that provided quite a minor spectacle, with sparks, for we watching airmen.

Floods at the rear of S.H.Q

24-HOUR GUARD

There were a number of carefully hushed-up suicide attempts – fortunately not always successful – for a variety of reasons that were obviously important to those desperate individuals concerned at the time. Commonest was the "Dear John" letter, always unexpected. For those driven far enough to attempt such an act, the easiest way was simply to walk out over the reef: the tide, currents and jagged, razor-sharp coral would between them pretty well guarantee the end – with permanent disappearance or eventual re-appearance further down the coast, unrecognisable.

One such case with which I was involved was when I was summoned to take my turn and stand twenty-four-hour guard at his sick-quarters bedside, over a huge individual who had walked out to the reef with obvious intentions but had been spotted by a male nursing orderly who, with great difficulty, had dragged him back. He was promptly drugged and bedded in sick quarters, but not strongly enough as it turned out. He awoke, still intent on topping himself and promptly walked out to the reef's edge again.

For a second time, the same nursing orderly went after him – against strict orders because of the obvious personal danger involved, so as well as saving the man's life for a second time, he was in trouble himself, although his first instinct had been to save life. The man was re-drugged, more potently the second time, and put to bed again in sick quarters, which was where I came in.

Although out for the count, he was still rather restless in disturbed sleep; each time he moved I nearly had kittens. I had to stay awake by his bedside throughout my twenty-four-hour stint, not the easiest marathon to completed in wide-awake mode; time of course went very slowly, even when broken by the occasional in situ meal break.

I have never been more relieved to finish a duty and hand over to the next luckless corporal than I was that day. I make two points about this incident: the nursing orderly who got into trouble for saving the same life twice was the same person I was later to hear whistling a bar from Brahms' Third at the taps; I also subsequently found out the sole reason for the attempted suicide: he hadn't received a letter from his mother for a fortnight. I'm a great believer in truth being stranger than fiction.

CHARACTERS

There were too many "characters" on the island to name or even remember them all. Just a few come most readily to mind, especially "Flit" Clayton – a Flight Sergeant, pilot of the tiny, all-white Auster bug-sprayer, who regularly took great pleasure in keeping us all fumigated, from hedge height (had there been any hedges). Wherever we tried to hide, he made sure his misty white spray would find us. If his ammunition did contain D.D.T., I'd hate to think of the state we might end up in, leave alone poor birds of prey you heard about in UK. If it was for freedom from mosquitoes, he must have done a fair job as I don't recall being bothered by these miniature blood-suckers – as I was indeed, with malarial results, on my next overseas tour in Singapore/Malaya three years later. Flies, however, were a different matter much of the time. Trust Flit to spring out on us unexpectedly: one minute you'd be peacefully minding your own business, when the next, Flit Clayton and his horrible little Auster, would be spray-bombing you from a suicidal low height. He was a character all right.

Another character, in a different way, was the replacement S.W.O. (Station Warrant Officer) who was responsible for routine discipline, and the less pleasant routine jobs that had to be done on the island. He replaced the previous S.W.O., who came out at about the same time as I did – an older man who should never have been sent out in such a situation – he was sent home quickly and quietly after a rapid breakdown. His replacement was a stroke of genius – a younger man, full of energy and good humour – tolerant and flexible and popular (for a S.W.O.). He organised things to suit the conditions at that time, including the Main Camp sewage disposal facility (not what we called it), a couple of miles away. Here, shifts of admin orderlies would disappear from human view for a fortnight or so, to re-appear when swapping over shifts, after complete isolation from the rest of the world, black as the ace of spades from their constant work outside in the unforgiving sun, and sometimes even sporting temporary beards until shaved off back in Main Camp. They did an important job, often unpleasant, in much less than salubrious conditions.

The adjacent H.Q. building to ours at airfield site was occupied by the Accounts Department – yes, we were paid! Now and then the Warrant Officer and Flight Sergeant there, who drove a Land Rover to and from work, would have a spare seat and would offer a lift to a stranded or late airman, back to

Main Camp. I thought this would be much more preferable to the usual rock-hard three-tonner until, riding with them one day, I was to change my mind when they performed one of their favourite party tricks – shared driving. Both sitting in the front, one would use the driving wheel and gear lever, the other the clutch and accelerator, and would swap over at will, with no warning. I never had complete faith in their co-ordination skills, so it was with mixed emotions if I was ever offered a lift by those two individuals when in party-trick mood: whether to take my life in their hands or to gratefully decline. Hobson's choice!

The same adj. who missed my typing error was also occasionally in the habit, especially with a captive audience to impress, of driving his Land Rover in the manner of a pilot – pre-flight-checking his aircraft with all the landing and take-off procedure patter, aloud to himself. To travel with him was a journey of mixed experiences. He also had a slightly unfortunate surname, which if you re-arranged a couple of vowels, would pose a rather coarse question!

SEXUAL ORIENTATION

Because of the concentration of literally thousands of servicemen suddenly thrown together, arriving and disappearing regularly as the tests developed, there were bound to be a small number of individuals, who in those less enlightened times, you could say were of uncertain gender, nowadays gay. You must appreciate that in the 1950s, and seventy years ago, there was much more of a taboo around this subject, and the M.O.D.s attitude was strict – considered necessary to Service morale (and morals?) and good order (discipline – a favourite military term); to root out any member of the Services on the island who was considered "active" and caught in what was deemed to be a compromising situation. These were considered a "bad risk" in our particular situation, and were quickly and quietly repatriated to the U.K.

Of course, we had our share of known effeminate young men who, without prejudice or making value judgments, were recognised by their mannerisms and occasionally keeping women's clothing in their lockers. They were tolerated and treated for what they were – companions and good friends in an often less than ideal situation, doing their jobs as well as anyone else. The official lids were kept tightly shut on this subject, so generally we knew very little apart from what went on in our own immediate living and working area.

As far as I knew, there was no anti-gay behaviour among the servicemen – just the occasional quiet disappearance back to U.K. Nowadays – how attitudes have changed – this whole area is treated sympathetically, sensibly and tolerantly, with much more understanding of gender issues and how society treats those who, in some ways were considered "different" in a sinister and immoral way fifty years ago.

FREE CIGARETTES

One day, an unexpected "treat" was presented to the island's smokers in the form of a huge packing case of some two million confiscated cigarettes, handed over as a good-will gift by H.M. Customs, and distributed equally to all ranks. This worked out at four hundred for each serviceman on the island – smoker and non-smoker. I quickly sold my share, making a small profit: there's a moral here somewhere. When I think back to how quickly those two million cigarettes went up in smoke, I'm afraid it lodges me, biased or not, more firmly than ever in the non-smoking lobby. I think the N.A.A.F.I. must have lost out on cigarette sales for a brief spell, but not for long if the number of daily smokers lounging on beach and in tents inhaling nicotine in between ale intake as a means of passing the time on this lonely nuclear outpost far from home, were any indication.

THE ARMY ON CHRISTMAS

Although the whole operation for the Christmas Island tests was very much a Joint Service effort, in my own experience we R.A.F. personnel had little close contact with the Army there. Despite the intensive co-operation between the Services at every level, there seemed little intermingling at Main Camp, apart from the occasional social shoulder-rubbing at leisure time and meals in the mess, at weekends and evenings, also in sports – especially soccer. We were, however, always aware of the tremendous amount of hard work under great pressure, that the Army Field Squadrons were doing in road and airfield construction and essential and maintenance services, invariably under very difficult and uncomfortable conditions.

Digging in the Debris – nothing much left after a tent burns down

We all shared the same location of course – the same Christmas Island conditions – but I would hazard a guess that, as I have said, individual personal experiences would be quite different. For one thing, the whole matter of their Army discipline regime was much tighter – more formal than our generally easier-going R.A.F. practice. The unnecessary lengths to which the

Army's daily "bull" routine were regularly taken, sometimes filtered through to us; their apparent need to have shining boots at all times, for instance, with inspections through the working day, even when employed in crushing coral rock with huge, dusty machines, and laying roads and airport runways in the heat and sweat of their 24-hour day; all seemed totally unrealistic to us. At night, when shift-working with the most arduous, dusty tasks, boots were inspected by torchlight. Even in the name of good Army order and discipline, surely this need not have been imposed in those circumstances?

Floods encountered on the way to work each day

Their tents were likewise rigidly "standardised" internally and externally – furniture to be painted in one compulsory colour, surrounding "gardens" bordered with coral block rows and neatly-raked sand. Haircuts were also inspected daily, at any time: woe betide any fancy variations to the short back and sides, given by Allan, my barber friend.

OFF-DUTY TIME

THE LAGOONS

What was there to do in the weekends, especially Sundays, when not on duty? Not a lot if your imagination wasn't stretched. Life here was at least in part largely a case of what you made of it – looking beyond the N.A.A.F.I. and drinking your cares away; sunbathing on the beach; patronising the Astra cinema. Yes, these were all very admirable, but horizons could always be widened, explored and filled with new experiences.

Christmas Island luxury cinema

I was a keen athlete, in particular, hammer-throwing and other field events, so I eventually sought out the Sports Store and discovered they actually had a hammer in stock. I looked around and found a space where I could practise safely, well away from human habitation, where my flying ball and chain would do no harm. This was obviously a solo event and not what you could call a majority sport; others could be shared with other like-minded individuals, like taking the weekend 3-tonner "taxi" to the lagoons for a day's swimming, fishing or simply wandering around this more remote area, nicely away from Main Camp and its weekend boredom. You could even have a go at throwing up whatever you could find that was suitable, at the palm trees, always loaded with ripe-looking and inviting coconuts, but rarely with success, being even more difficult to dislodge than off the coconut shy at a U.K. fairground. I even learnt to climb coconut trees, in bare feet or plimsolls, but only those that were slightly less than vertical, and only in my madder moments.

I started up a Music Club, which took care of at least one evening a week, after discovering a small stock of L.P.s and an old record-player, hidden away and dust-covered in the Education Section. I had long been a keen photographer, so my camera usually came with me most places I went (although this habit cost me dear when I left it on a distant beach one foraging day; it wasn't there when my memory returned and I went to look for it, so I had to send by mail order for a replacement from Hong Kong). It provided a useful visual record of much of my island stay.

Eventually some weights and lifting equipment appeared in the Main Camp at the far end of the tent lines, and gradually a clientele of regular weightlifters and bodybuilders soon grew to take advantage of this small but well-organised facility, a welcome addition to our leisure time activities. There were the inevitable rough and ready soccer and other pitches on the way to the lagoons – popular and well-patronised with regular tournaments – but players had to be careful not to fall and sustain cuts that so often failed to heal properly and would readily turn septic despite great efforts to sluice them down after the game.

Balloon fish from the lagoon

The lagoons, another long, bumpy ride from Main Camp, were very extensive, forming the wide claw-shaped northern part of the island, but most of us never strayed further than the main swimming area – not, I'm afraid, the usual movie-goer's picture of a romantic, clear blue beach and ocean-fringed swimmers' paradise – instead, rather quite a shallow, featureless "lake", with a thick layer of soft, slimy coral mud that oozed underfoot; very salty, with virtually no beach. A diving platform was provided further out in the slightly deeper parts – but still too shallow for proper diving – the only facility to be found here. It did, however, double as an access raft for less-strong swimmers, and simply for messing about on and off.

The 3-tonner "taxi" service took us there and back (a long walk for those who missed the last one back in the early evening), along largely unmade, compacted coral tracks, and through dried, peeling coral mud that covered most of the island, constantly having to weave in and out between low bushes, land crabs and the scattered groves of coconut palms, in various stages of growth, from sprouting nuts scattered on the ground with no visible means of support or nourishment, to forty-plus feet giants, some leaning at crazy angles in the sparse coral "soil". Many acres of flat, nondescript scrub with an uneven sprinkling of palms surrounded the lagoons on three sides, but most were little visited in my experience, apart from the occasional adventurous angler or enthusiastic birdwatcher.

My own fishing trophies numbered just one and a half – a small pufferfish and almost a stingray. The pufferfish is not built for speed, especially when it ballooned itself if it felt threatened, so my catch was no great shakes. The stingray was different. I had found a discarded iron fishing spear one day, and finders was keepers. It had a flattened, slightly barbed point at one end. We were paddling one weekend in the shallow, oozy-bottomed lagoon in not much more than thigh-depth, when the ray slowly glided into view. I shouted excitedly to my friends and began stalking the brute. It was by no means a giant, but still quite a decent size. When at last within striking distance, and feeling fortunate that I'd managed to approach it so far without arousing its suspicions, I struck downwards with the spear, pinioning its wing. It thrashed about wildly for several agonising seconds, with me hanging on for dear life to my potential trophy, then suddenly tore itself free, flashed away across the lagoon and disappeared, leaving me not quite proud owner of a more notable catch. I only hope it recovered from my attempt to convert it into sting-ray steaks.

By the lagoon

A shark net had at some time previously been stretched across the main swimming lagoon entrance, but if the occasional but persistent rumour of a distinctive fin seen breaking the surface were true, not much use, especially in its neglected state. Just in case there was a chance of any of them lurking around and "available", some of us bought large metal shark hooks from the new N.A.A.F.I. shop in an attempt to bag such an ambitious trophy (ignoring all the other implications involved in such a capture). I never heard of a catch being made.

I bought one such hook – about six to eight inches long and about a quarter of an inch thick, and one Sunday with nothing better to do, baited it with something appropriate – I can't remember exactly what it was, but it wasn't human – tied it with some stout rope to a large bush at the water's edge, and left it there optimistically, before returning to Main Camp. Next time I returned, of course it had disappeared, most likely by another shark-hunter, who would probably have had no more luck than I. If only I could have used a traditional Gilbertese iron-wood hook, grown with magic, baited with magic and cast into the lagoon with magic, that Arthur Grimble had so vividly described in his "A Pattern of Islands", I might have had more pagan luck than with more modern "civilised" angling techniques.

Bonefish off the beach

On the way to our weekend lagoons, along the less frequently used crushed coral roads, were to be found the occasional mysterious signposts, at the odd road junction, whose unfamiliar place-names – SPAL, PARIS, PORT – fascinated me. SPAL, for instance, I learnt later, had been a real airline, composed of little more than a small hotel and airstrip, derelict since "Grapple" took over the whole island and any chance of commercial success – South Pacific Airlines. I never managed to reach any of these places; I wish I could have satisfied my curiosity though, to see for myself what they looked like. For such a small island, it contained so much of the unknown to the vast majority of its temporary inhabitants, although some officers had the use of small motorbikes.

Swimming weekends in the lagoons could sometimes be supplemented by a longer drive to Port London, where the naval supply vessels docked and discharged their cargoes. The journey to the Port was a longer, even bumpier ride in the standard three-tonner "taxi", with not a great deal going on there when you eventually arrived, apart from the usual swim, very similar to the less distant lagoons, but a bit of a change. I only went there once or twice, as numbers seemed to be restricted (one three-tonner load?), with limited activity time before your return transport left for Main Camp, but still a reasonable place to play around in the warm waters.

Gilbertese

Most parts of the Port were out of bounds to us, including the picturesque Gilbertese village, in its idyllic setting, which housed the native workers and their families in traditional palm thatch, stilted houses. They came from the widely scattered islands of the old Gilbert and Ellis group and Line Islands, of which Christmas Island was an isolated northern outlier. Originally working the coconut plantations, they now laboured for their Grapple masters, mainly at the Port. Their houses were clustered around the Manaeba – traditional communal meeting house, a wonderfully designed structure for maximum space, shade and ventilation.

One day I had the chance, out of the blue, of a helicopter flight – a practice rescue mission, I think, off Port London. This was a new experience for me. We took off from the main airfield, in what I found to be a relatively noisy, draughty and vibrating machine, compared with a fixed-wing aircraft, but it was exciting to fly slowly, almost in the open air, and take in the scenery below, from a relatively low height. During the flight, my luck was in: I spotted a large yellow sand shark and a manta ray – these made my day.

MUSIC CLUB

After a few weeks on the island, I was beginning to have withdrawal symptoms of a sort – I'd heard no classical music on this barren atoll since leaving U.K. I took myself to the Main Camp Education Section (there was one, even on Christmas Island) to see what I could discover. I asked the Education Officer, an affable Flight Lieutenant, if there was any stock of L.P.s anywhere around and, if possible, something on which to play them. My luck was in; he was helpful and later produced a small Deccalian record-player, ageing and dusty, and eventually located a small pile of 12-inch L.P. classical records in an equally dusty box, also untouched since its arrival on the island. I told him I would like to start up a Music Club; he was enthusiastic and agreed to issue the lot on long-term loan; he included the use of the Education Section as venue, at one evening a week. This was the beginning of a happy improvement to my life here, making things a little more bearable on that one evening a week, and a change from the Astra. Fortunately, the choice of music, although of limited amount, was a fairly eclectic mix of well-known symphonies with some shorter and less familiar works: a good potential for widening one's musical horizons.

The Music Club, duly formed, attracted a small but gradually increasing clientele of like-minded islanders, where rank was no barrier. We could take the record-player outside where the evenings were a little cooler, with more space, and occasionally, spectacularly beautiful sunsets. After a while we somehow acquired more L.P.s, shipped from U.K. Our high point came when an enthusiastic club member, a young Royal Engineers Army Captain, offered to ship out is hi-fi equipment from U.K., and he was as good as his word. When it arrived – magic! – what a fantastic difference it made to our symphonic sounds; we never looked back.

Another musical highlight that stands out in my memory was playing a complete performance of Handel's Messiah, played at the right time of year, to quite a large audience, against the familiar, balmy backdrop of breaking surf over the reef, off the beach less than a hundred yards away. It was a small oasis of calm on a large island all too often lacking that vital quality.

At Christmas time, a Gilbertese choir was assembled at Main Camp; they gave us the rare treat of their versions of well-known carols, interspersed with some of their own traditional songs. To hear this joyful, enthusiastic sound, among the swaying palms, with the usual muted swish of the nearby surf, it really did give the assembled audience a truly memorable impression of a more serene tropical atmosphere.

Another fleeting musical moment, that still holds magic for me whenever I recall it today, happened in the most incongruous of places – the communal "washhouse" – rows of taps, piping and long metal sinks where we washed, shaved and scoured the scrapings from our metal mess-trays. I was washing my hands alone at these taps one day, when I became aware of another person at the other end, unnoticed at first. He was whistling a short snatch from the first movement of Brahms' third symphony – just three notes – several times over. This didn't really register for a few seconds and in the meantime the whistler had quietly disappeared before I could speak to him. I did recognise him as a Corporal Nursing Orderly from Sick Quarters, whom I knew only slightly, from my frightening twenty-four-hour guard on the attempted suicide; it was the one who saved a life twice over. Without fail, each time I hear those three notes now, I'm immediately transported back to those taps, complete with phantom whistler.

Incredibly, after so many recent attempts to contact possible island acquaintances on Forces Reunited via my computer, I did make a breakthrough with this missing whistling orderly. I had constantly remembered his surname and RAF trade, and suddenly there were his details on the screen in front of me. We exchanged emails, confirming that it was indeed he who had twice dragged the attempted suicide from the reef. However, he has no memory of me or the 'taps' incident, which is hardly surprising when you come to think of it. Although this was my own acute personal memory, it was a one-way event – for me rather than him. Even so, this in no way dims the magic of that moment in time.

THE ASTRA

One of the few evening diversions we could enjoy regularly on the island was a visit to the Astra Cinema. Cinema? Forget the resplendent art-deco edifices we were used to, to sit back and relax in plush red comfort in U.K. – ours here was different – but still an institution. Our Astra was a roughly circular, sandy-floored open-air stockade, originally surrounded by neat Hessian panels about eight feet high, but by now replete with gaps and gaping holes. You couldn't pass the Astra in the light of day without feeling a sense of shame at its state of extreme dilapidation. There were seats, of course, if you could call them seats. If you paid a shilling (five pence in new money) there were rough scaffolding boards to sit on, supported by telegraph pole sections buried in the sand. For those pretentious people we plebs called the Barons, there were, further back, the luxury of folding metal chairs, hardly any more comfortable than our boards, and priced at two shillings (ten pence new money). We lads never aspired to these though – they were for the higher ranks – we knew our place! The rather mobile canvas screen would sometimes tend to billow in and out in waves with the constant sea breezes, giving the term "motion pictures" a new meaning. I suppose the selection of films was reasonable enough, and as we enjoyed Hobson's choice, we simply accepted them and sat back.

Looking back, however, the most bizarre part of the evening's entertainment was our prior sartorial preparation. Our clothing was dependent on three factors – the weather, the need to dress in something legal other than our daily K.D. outfit, and to be comfortable during the performance whatever the weather. The minimum uniform we could get away with were our K.D. trousers (longs only, at night – shorts not allowed) but there it ended. We donned our short-sleeved tropical issue pyjamas (nice shade of pale blue!), our feet in cool flip-flops. Because the Astra was completely open to whatever kind of weather happened to be occurring at the time of performance, we wore our jungle hats and took our monsoon ponchos if there was any chance of rain, which came in only one size – tropical downpour. To complete the outfit, a pillow, to make those planks a little more tolerable to our tender behinds. To coin a phrase, to put the icing on the cake, and complete our assorted baggage we would stop at the Mess to fill our white pint mugs with steaming cocoa. Thus attired and equipped, we duly paid our shillings, entered our Astra stockade and sat down, as prepared for any eventuality as we could be.

Only occasionally did it rain hard enough to make viewing a chore – then we just hunched down under our ponchos and jungle hats, neither of which were fully waterproof, and let the rain drip steadily from us, seeping on to our trousers and eventually our poor pillows, which somehow had to dry out before we took ourselves to bed that night. Very rarely was a performance cancelled for a severe downpour or for technical problems. It must have been that stiff upper lip again that made us sit there and endure such uncomfortable conditions –we were, though, a genuinely captive audience.

As I recall, the loudest, most spontaneous cheer I ever heard during any Astra performance oddly enough, was not for the appearance of a scantily clad female, but during a film about Captain Cook's voyages, when he was reading aloud from the ship's log. It went something like this: "Christmas Eve, 1777, discovered a solitary coral atoll today, very near the Equator, which we have named "Christmas Island". The noise – cheers and jeers – was deafening for quite a while.

COVER-UP

A situation that arose quite spontaneously during my stay on the island, which could have turned unpleasant had it not been handled by the Commanding Officer with sensitivity, care and humour, was the subject of certain aspects of leisure-time sunbathing. Climate-wise, the environment was ideal – plenty of sun without being too unpleasantly hot, sea breezes to lessen its apparent severity, miles of sandy beach nearby and enough spare time for a spot or two of sun-worship, especially at weekends. The sexes were, on the island, rather unequally balanced – thousands of men and just two women – W.V.S. ladies of indeterminate age – whom we met rarely away from our occasional contact at their canteen workplace – there being no N.A.A.F.I. shop yet at the time. We felt that they must move in higher circles than we lower ranks, not that this mattered to us.

One Sunday morning

At any hour of the day, mainly at weekends, unless you were a shift-worker, large numbers of steadily browning bodies of varying shades, could be seen, ranging from pure white – we called them "moonies" – through degrees of pinkness, getting there via the inevitable burn-peel-burn-peel process, or wonderful shades of brown to almost black for the old hands. All new arrivals were a paler shade of British temperate zone off-white, so everyone else called them "moonies" as I mentioned, until the novelty wore off or another batch arrived to tease. When they were no longer "moonies" themselves, it became their turn to catcall the latest new "recruits", and so the cycle continued.

Some of the regular sunbathers, however, preferred an all-over tan and sunbathed naked. It didn't matter to anyone: if you were of modest make-up, you'd look the other way or sun-bathe elsewhere. If you came across the occasional naked body engaging in the practice of active sun-worship with religious zeal, this was a fairly common sight, and no problem. However, the two W.V.S. ladies sometimes took their off-duty stroll along these same stretches of beach occupied by the ad hoc nudists and for some reason complained to higher authority.

Relaxing off duty

All Service matters on the island rested on the broad shoulders of the Commanding Officer, and this complaint was duly brought to his attention. What was he to do? The sexes were not what you would call equally balanced; the lads were off duty and doing no-one any harm except to the sensitivities of those two ladies, who weren't forced to patrol those particular beaches anyhow. Faced with this delicate situation, he had to take some kind of action – to be sympathetic to the feelings of the W.V.S. ladies, but not be too heavy-handed with threats or direct orders to the otherwise innocent sun-bathers. His solution was simple, effective and generally acceptable to both sides. He issued a special request in Station Routine Orders, which ran something like this: "It has long been a good Service tradition, that equipment not needed for immediate use should be stored away neatly, out of sight until needed. In other words, wear shorts." It worked.

COCONUTS HOME

As coconuts did literally grow on trees on the island, and these trees were in great abundance, found almost everywhere, there was usually a plentiful supply of this raw material. But what could we do with this ready resource? Exotic, and of enough novelty value to delight our families back home, why didn't we send some home? We sometimes did, but first we had to make them suitable for sending through the post. First was the difficult task of removing the outer husk to reduce weight and size. Easy enough for a native Polynesian with generations of practice, parang and hard sharp stake on which to lever off its coir husk. More difficult for we British amateurs though. We did somehow manage this job, with the selection of ad hoc "tools", often an education to behold. Guaranteed to increase our sweat levels, we considered it worth the effort for the novelty value to our beloved relations back home. Then we'd paint the hard, dark brown casing white to take the address and hopefully the stamps, and B.F.P.O. would kindly do the rest.

Frank Craig shinning up a tree

PARTIES

Excuses for the occasional celebration were not hard to think up. Raw material for these events – canned beer and other alcohols – were freely available to buy at the N.A.A.F.I., Sergeants' and Officers' Messes. Birthdays were the commonest excuse, especially twenty-firsts; Christmas time, New Year, even on receiving "Dear Johns" or similar letters; promotion, or of course, for no particular reason at all – a spontaneous Saturday night booze-up for us. These could either be in the N.A.A.F.I. compound, on the beach, or, unofficially, in our tents, when elastic sides and loud noise were the main requirements. To say they were often riotous without becoming completely out of hand, was to state the obvious. Standard "uniform" comprised lurid Hawaiian shirts, K.D. longs and flip-flops. The pile of "dead" cans and other rubbish littering venue tables and floors next morning was unbelievable – how we managed to tidy our tents with severe hangovers, I can't remember.

Peter Harrison's 21st birthday party

These common events were, as in U.K., a vital safety-valve for our less than perfect life, in our case imposed exile on this far-flung dot in mid-Pacific, thousands of miles away from mums, dads, brothers, sisters, wives, babies, children, friends, and others. Homesickness was often rife but usually well controlled, with only occasional severe emotional outbursts (including the rare suicide attempt I've already mentioned).

Xmas party 1957

Parties never did any harm except to those teetotallers who were trying to sleep next door, or shift-workers whose unsocial hours weren't our (or their) fault any way. Those senior ranks on duty inevitably turned a blind eye to loud parties, except in extenuating circumstances, which were rare.

New Years celebrations S.A.D.O

Examples I vividly recall included Pete Harrison's twenty-first, Christmas and New Year celebrations in our tent, and the token Christmas office party at the old airfield site Headquarters, when all ranks in a particular Section mixed and drank socially for a short while, and certain officers briefly became more human.

At this uncustomary informal "party", the invisible but tangible distancing between officers and other ranks (with poor S.N.C.O.s somewhere in between), did not altogether disappear, even for the duration of the party, which was brief but pleasant. I remember, however, at this particular gathering, one of the officers serving us, asked if there were any complaints; one of the airmen was incautious enough to reply with a pig grunt, for which he was charged with offensive conduct. I accept that some barriers are just meant not to be broken in the Services, even at role-reversal events like office Christmas parties; generally, the officers were human beings most of the time –some more so than others!

C.O. cutting cake at New Year

A different kind of party obviously occurred when two fellow corporals "disappeared" while on leave in Fiji; how they managed this I never discovered – and they missed the plane back: something about the Fijian beach at night and friendly local women. As far as I remember, not a lot in the way of discipline came of this event, but much secret envy from the rest of us.

WILDLIFE

With the time and the inclination to explore beyond the overcrowded Main Camp, beyond even the swimming lagoons, the island's non-human wildlife was well worth finding and watching, especially the birds, usually no more difficult than walking inland for a mile or two to the extensive and largely deserted lagoon margins, where low scrub sprouted a selection of various-sized sea-birds, adults and young, on very basic twig nests about a metre above the ground. The chicks perched like out-of-scale fluffy tumours on top of those pint-sized bushes – the only available off-ground nesting accommodation on this low-lying atoll.

Frank Craig in Port London Lagoon

Any weekend was suitable for a foray inland, except if spoilt by heavy rain, and you were never disappointed. Despite my general ignorance of Pacific ornithology, I could identify frigate birds, boobies (two types – red-footed and blue-footed), and fairy terns to be the commonest. They were virtually fearless, having no reason to be otherwise at that time, as few Servicemen ever ventured far from the safe swimming lagoons.

Frank Craig jumping at Port London Lagoon

My most pleasurable memories were or those snowy-white fairy terns with their black dot eyes, hovering over us, just above our heads, only half-disturbed if you made no sudden movements. They were also most photogenic. The large, ungainly but fearless chicks, especially of frigate birds and boobies, would spread and flap their untidy patchwork wings and hiss and squeak with large, open, out-of-scale beaks, beady eyes and woolly heads, if they thought that they were being threatened in any way, then settle back when we had passed, pretending we hadn't just been by; a glazed but satisfied look in their eyes, I'm certain.

View of the safe area from the guard tower

Sunday at the Lagoons

A properly organised Ornithologists Club was evidently formed some time after I left, as I have seen one of their impressive magazines since. In 1957 I had no idea how many species were to be found on the island, but today, Christmas Island is an ornithologists' paradise of world renown.

Fledgling Frigate bird

Meanwhile, back at Main Camp, the occasional Gilbertese pie-dog, cat or kitten was to be found, loosely "adopted" by a tent's occupants, while they bothered to stay. I did see, at close quarters, kittens with an extra two toes on each paw – an odd sight. I wondered how this mutation had come about. Perhaps some sort of inter-breeding while being with the Gilbertese living and working on the island, or, dare I wonder, as a result of nuclear fall-out contamination?

Native kittens (note seven toes)

Island wildlife of much greater nuisance value, and subject of long and fierce debate, arguments and complaint over how to deal with or at least reduce their numbers (besides running over as many of them as possible), were the land-crabs. They were so numerous as to be found swarming literally everywhere, especially where you didn't want them to be at the time.

Land-crabs could be quite nippy (sorry) scuttlers if they were in the mood, but usually their gait was deliberately slow, careful and hesitant, as though plotting every sideways step several moves ahead like scheming chess-players, as if unsure if they were in the right place at that particular time of day. They were always on the defensive with their unequal claws. The smaller one, much the more powerful, I discovered, was used for defence, attack and eating; the larger for display and bravado. Their rather lop-sided appearance was accentuated by their sideways gait.

They could be cornered against any tussock of tall grass, when they would fiddle and dribble fiercely, drawing their claws defensively in front of their bodies as if half-expected to raise a dissonant scrape on hidden violins. Their flattened corpses were to be found, covered with flies if fresh, just about everywhere, especially on the main road between Main Camp and Airfield sites where, so numerous, it was very difficult to avoid them with a three-ton Bedford truck – commonest form of transport for men and supplies alike. Also, the ubiquitous, invariably clapped-out Land Rovers, used by senior N.C.O.s and officers who had to be mobile, and of course, M.T. drivers, whose job it was any way.

Swimming lagoon with raft

The crabs would invade our tents at the drop of a hat, any time of day or night: the "crab-proof" plank of wood at each tent entrance, wasn't always effective. They had to be ejected by whoever at the time was the bravest, nearest, daftest, or whoever first came across the particular crustacean, if their anger outdid their fear. A few of us learnt to handle land-crabs: it helped to be aware of the range limitations of claw movement – about a 180 degree sweep to the front only. Because their hydraulics weren't flexible enough to reach behind, if you picked one up carefully by its sides from behind, and kept faith with this piece of useful expertise, it was powerless to nip the holder. However, once in your hand, you could use the frustrated crustacean to scare your friends by lunging towards them, crab nippers outstretched angrily, spitting and dribbling with impotent rage. I'm afraid I was one of these teasers, but rarely did the fit take me to show off my questionable skill.

Can't rest in peace in my nest

Occasionally, we also tried to race them, and painted numbers on their backs, but we might as well have been racing uncooperative snails for the chance of anything like a realistic race being completed. One day I experimented with the comparative power of small and large claws: this was amply demonstrated when the small pincer almost crushed a wooden ruler "borrowed" from the office, while the large one hardly dented it. By and large, land-crabs were an inevitable feature of Christmas Island life, to be treated with extreme caution, unwillingly tolerated, hated, deliberately run over, kicked out of your tent in disgust, complained about constantly; even used as a terror tool by a reckless few; generally to be kept at more than arm's length, I would say.

The rats were a different kettle of fish, to mix my metaphors. They were nocturnal but fairly common. They were a darned nuisance when we were trying to get to sleep: they could often be heard scurrying across a dark tent floor mat. They were occasionally known to scuttle over a recumbent form, not always asleep, a very unpleasant experience. This led to a series of complaints to higher authority, ultimately reaching the lofty corridors of M.O.D. London. The eventual reaction of this remote authority was not popular with the men in their tents at night with these rampant rodents. Their reply was that these small, harmless furry creatures were not rats at all – simply jerboas (but desert rats all the same). This cut no ice with us at the time, but what else could we tiny cogs do within such a complex military wheel?

Next worm please

Perhaps the most efficient wildlife survivor globally, in the insect world at least, was the humble cockroach. Although this ubiquitous insect abounded on the island, as everywhere, I didn't notice them much; perhaps if I'd been a cook in the Airmen's Mess, it would have been a different story. However, there was one brief but frightening moment of encounter – the only time I ever saw one fly. I had to visit an infrequently used paper store, in a small, stuffy and unventilated room. As I opened the door and switched on the light to see my way, this apparition suddenly rose from its hiding place among those assorted reams, and flew straight at me, with a horrible whirring of wings. I don't like cockroaches at the best of times – they scuttle far too quickly for me – but this one was different: it was flying straight at me. Like a shot, leaving a pile of freshly dropped bricks on the floor behind me, and with a strangled cry, I fled that stuffy paper store, leaving it to the flying horror and its equally nasty friends. I didn't think that paper was so important any more, at least to me. Let someone else get zapped! I don't mind spiders – except the big, fast ones – and I don't admit to being a coward generally, but I drew the line at large, flying cockroaches that day.

I could round off "wildlife" with flies and bedbugs, both mentioned elsewhere, and in my opinion, not worth another mention!

~

Going back to nature was not altogether unrelated to other island "wildlife". One weekend, quite spontaneously, three of us mates decided to "go native" in the lagoons next day. On the Sunday, dressed in bathers, we set off for the more distant, remote lagoons. We took with us some tins of soup, newspaper and matches to start a fire, a spear for fishing (and teasing birds), and ourselves. We just went for a longer than usual walk, then simply "went native". Well away from civilisation, and other human life, we collected driftwood on the narrow coral beach, took off our bathers, lit a fire by the water's edge, heated and drank our soup straight from the can, paddled and swam afterwards, lounging in the warm, shallow salt water, feeling the squidgy sand ooze between our toes. We pranced around for a while, struck some silly poses, took each other's photographs, found some feathers and stuck them in our hair, and finally replaced our bathers.

Frank Craig with twigs on his head

We frightened some innocent nesting birds perched atop the low-lying scrub, minding their own business, then slowly wandered back towards civilisation and other human life. This had been a spontaneous idea, to fill one boring Sunday's leisure-time, to relieve the too-frequent ennui of doing the same old thing most weekends. It had worked a treat – I suppose it may seem to have been a slightly risqué action to some, but it was merely an ad hoc day's outing on our own modern desert island, between three good friends – Eddie, Geoff and me. Here we were, flung together in a less then pleasant land and not at all eccentric when you come to think of it and, in context, we thought, like our evening cinema, dressed-up jaunts – nothing out of the ordinary to us.

On the beach trying to feed the local birds

THE GILBERTESE AND GRIMBLE

A more friendly, loveable, unassuming, happy group of people never walked the earth, as far as I'm concerned: the local Gilbertese Islanders, who worked mainly at Port London, and lived in their picturesque village there with their families. We servicemen met them mainly when they descended on our Main Camp on a Sunday morning, by the busload, to attend one of our two island coral-block and atap churches which adjoined each-other on the seaward edge of our Main Camp, just on top of the narrow beach, only feet above sea-level

Flogger of Gilbertese souvenirs

These two churches had been hand-built of local coral stones – the C. of E. of St. Nicholas by the Rev. Alsopp and a group of dedicated servicemen in 1956-57 - and were surprisingly well-attended. To say these folk were friendly was a wonderful understatement – their broad smiles always lit up their likewise broad faces, except maybe, for only the smallest children and babies, who would gaze at us in silent wonder with wide, dark eyes, as if asking who these strange, pale people were. I don't know why, but they always brought with them, especially the women and older girls, what may have been their most treasured domestic possessions – chattels, such as aluminium teapots and the like – or ordinary, every-day objects to us.

Gilbertese village in Port London

Sunday morning church service

They were all of stocky build, just below average height, with flashing white teeth and smiles to match. They wore ordinary, every-day clothes – a nice mix of their traditional dress and the European garb the enthusiastic but misguided Victorian missionaries had imposed upon these happy, pagan islanders a century or more ago. On the way from the parked buses that brought them to the churches, a distance of less than fifty yards, were our showers and toilets. The showers were absolutely basic; the toilet "block" similarly endowed but as dilapidated and originally surrounded as our Astra cinema – ragged Hessian, with a now open-plan character all their own. Comprising a row of a dozen back-to-back chemical toilets, they originally enjoyed a degree of privacy to back and sides with Hessian sheets nailed between posts but completely open at the front – there were only we male servicemen on the island, so this lack of privacy didn't really matter.

Church of England Church – Main Camp

By the time I had arrived, these rather flimsy divisions were not shall we say, in their original pristine state, becoming progressively more tattered and neglected – and more and more open – so less and less private – something that, as I have said, didn't particularly matter to us. Neither, evidently, did it bother those gregarious Gilbertese – men, women or children – who lacked modesty even more than we did. More than once did I feel an urgent call of nature on a Sunday morning (the food usually guaranteed this), requiring me to assume a sitting position within what was left of the Hessian. While here, minding my own business, I could suddenly find myself joined by a friendly, smiling Gilbertese woman, who might then engage me in happy conversation via smiles, gestures and a few words of English, while sitting on the next toilet. This tended to be just a little disconcerting at first, but you soon got used to it! I felt it was best to pretend that we British did this kind of thing all the time – nothing out of the ordinary – after all, didn't we as a nation survive and thrive with typical sangfroid and stiff upper lips? I'm wondering if we even also occasionally shared a toilet roll – something else at times, conspicuous by its absence.

Just one or two of the Gilbertese men, one in particular, were the Mid-Pacific equivalent of Arthur Daly or Del Boy – wheeler-dealers who would offer us locally-made souvenirs. Especially popular were shark-teeth swords made from closely-woven palm leaves and tiny, serrated teeth – sharp as needles. To me, one of these was a must-have souvenir, so, after the usual bartering with the Gilbertese Del Boy, I became the proud owner of one of these collectable items. When time came to return home, I found that, while packing all my worldly island goods into one (or was it two?) canvas kit-bags, the awkwardly-shaped and needle-sharp sword wouldn't fit in, so I asked a friend who was going back on the same flight, to pack it in his less- than-full suitcase, and I would reclaim it at Lyneham on landing. Of course, I forgot in the rush, and the near fatal flight aftermath. So did he and I never saw that precious sword again. I suppose you live and learn, sometimes the hard way.

Small cowrie shells were another favourite, I remember, made into a wonderful variety of local ornaments, as well as coral of different sizes, types and colours, unadorned, or made into knick-knacks.

Christmas carol service by Gilbertese

The Gilbertese also fielded a superb choir (another, but happier result of those missionaries?) on the rare occasion, especially at Christmas, when they would sit in a wide half-circle and sing wonderful songs, carols and other hymns, to a large, appreciative audience, with again the constant muted accompaniment of the surf in the background, breaking over the reef. The atmosphere was serene and almost heavenly for a moment in time.

Gilbertese leaving R.C. church

I'm not sure which event triggered the other on the island – meeting the Gilbertese, or discovering Arthur Grimble's wonderfully evocative book: "A Pattern of Islands" and its sequel: "Return to the Islands". I suppose they happened pretty well at the same time, but the books certainly left a lasting impression on my mind, memory and outlook, of the history of the Pacific Islands and their peoples. "A Pattern of Islands" was written in 1952 by a man who had gone through the old Colonial Service, from young Assistant District Officer to Commissioner in the British Pacific Islands, earlier in the last century. After many years, he retired, with a history of chronic dysentery, and wrote a few short articles for various magazines, with reminiscences of his life's work in the Pacific. These were later gathered together and compiled into his book, soon after which he was commissioned by the B.B.C. to record some of these adventures, which quickly caught the listening public's imagination. His superb command of English, extensive vocabulary employed with poetic effect in his empathetic descriptions of the islands and their peoples, led to the book being adopted as a standard G.C.S.E. English text. He was especially sympathetic to the islanders' culture, history, religion and ways of life, much of which had been stifled and forcibly changed (mostly for the worse), by high-minded but well-meaning, misguided Victorian missionaries.

Christmas Island was a Line Islands outlier of the Gilbert and Ellis Group, which eventually became independent and has since changed its name to Kiribati. I read and re-read the two books, particularly those sections that most caught my imagination, using them extensively in my final English dissertation when training to be a Geography teacher in 1966, after I left the R.A.F.

PERKS

Working as a Headquarters clerk could have its advantages at times, especially if you kept your ear to the ground. I managed three visits to Oahu, Hawaii, each in different circumstances, with an official duty, a "perk" and a brief transit through on my way back home. The first was a three-day "temporary duty" for three of us – clerks from S.H.Q. – to sort out the filing system at the tiny R.A.F. Air Transport Detachment at Hickam Air Base, Honolulu, where the contents of their office filing cabinets had reached a chaotic state. I took another corporal, Dennis, and an S.A.C., Dave, with me to see, between us, what improvement we could make. Because we were there on duty, we were paid the local overseas allowance (L.O.A.) - a paltry sum per day even then, but it helped to keep us mobile in Oahu for a couple of days.

Honolulu at night

The job itself turned out to be straightforward enough to enable we experienced clerks to sort the whole lot out within the first twenty-four hours, leaving the rest of our brief stay free to wander at large on Oahu.

Old cobbler at Honolulu

We promptly made the most of our lightning stopover, starting with a quick tour of the huge air base at Hickam, our host for the duration. The breadth of facilities for its American servicemen was fantastic to we Limeys, and took us a while to take it all in. We then let ourselves loose in Honolulu town, almost penniless apart from our day's L.O.A., but happy.

Hickam Air Force Base December 1957

Billeted with the U.S.A.F. at Hickam for our stay, our light, airy huts were surrounded by much greenery and gorgeous displays of red and yellow hibiscus, Hawaii's national flower: they grew everywhere on the island, almost like weeds! We were also fed and watered courtesy of the U.S.A.F., to a standard that would have ordinarily kept us within camp bounds –a huge, fascinating air base of so many facilities – had there not been so many other wonderful diversions on the island that we couldn't miss the once-in-a-lifetime chance to experience. The quality and quantity, for instance, of food suddenly available and laid before us in the Airmens' Mess, was incredible, especially so because of the general standard (or lack of it) of what we were used to on Christmas. For instance, the sliced bread on all tables we couldn't believe – pure, brilliant white, thinly sliced, with the consistency of softest sponge. When we filed past the servery, the sea of fried eggs and bacon gently sizzling on huge, square griddles, seemed unreal. We were asked, for the first time in my case, whether we wanted our eggs (plural) "sunny side up" or "over-easy"? We actually had a choice! Needless to say, we ate here whenever we could. The variety of sauces and other condiments on every table was also a sight to behold, complementing the superb selection of milks and other soft drinks on display, freely available to all. No wonder so many of our transatlantic cousins tend towards overweight.

Hickam Air Force Base December 1957

Our tour of the huge air base proved to be one of the longest walks we'd had for a long time. Its facilities seemed endless – we liked the forces' N.A.A.F.I. shop – the P.X. (Post Exchange) store: full of discounted goods like L.P. records, electrical goods – in fact just like a small supermarket today. There were at least three swimming pools on the base – we were allowed to use the other-ranks' pool, itself of super size and facilities. Goodness knows what the other two (for S.N.C.O.s and officers) were like. So, we swam and played around, then posed in turn on the high diving board – just for the record. One of the first things we did on reaching Honolulu was to have a drink at one of the many bars dotted round town. When we entered, the bartender looked us over curiously, for several moments, and then asked us if we were from Germany? After we quickly put him right, we asked him why he thought we were Germans. He replied he'd been looking for some kind of identification feature of our nationality, something like a lapel badge, and not seeing any, assumed we were Germans! After everything was nicely resolved, he gave us drinks on the house – suitable compensation for a case of mistaken identity.

At Hickam Air Force Base

The U.S. certainly knew how to look after its servicemen serving overseas. Every Christmas a bevy of top showbiz personalities were flown out to

Hawaii from San Francisco, in time to give the U.S. Forces in the Pacific a terrific Christmas Show at the famous Pearl Harbour naval base, in its huge theatre called the Bloch Arena. We were given tickets for this 1957 event at the R.A.F. Detachment, when collecting our day's L.O.A., so we made our way there, in uniform (compulsory) to Pearl Harbour, later that day. Walking through the base in the early evening there were still many shell pockmarks clearly to be seen on the old concrete barrack blocks, from that fateful day in World War II, since painted over and preserved for posterity as a visual reminder of this pivotal event. The Bloch Arena was huge, even by American standards and was heaving, wall to wall, with thousands of U.S. servicemen – sailors, soldiers and airmen, plus three rather embarrassed British airmen in K.D., trying to look invisible or at least inconspicuous in our seats amid a sea of smart tan and white. The stars were well over an hour late leaving San Francisco with local weather problems there postponing departure, and arrived an hour late for their show.

On Paradise leave

To fill in time in what we were about to learn was their traditional way, there was audience participation, directed by the resident compere. He would ask in turn, who, in that vast audience, was from, say, Texas, and at various points in the sea of faces, all Texans would stand and cheer themselves, crowing and whooping as they did so, arms raised in self-salute – no inhibitions! This dialogue went on for quite a while – state after state, city after city, taking their turns to stand, wave and howl acknowledgement, in ever-more competing manner, encouraged by the rest of the audience. Interspersed, as expected, were the sprinkling of usual ad hoc jokes. Inevitably, I suppose, it had to be our turn sometime, and here it came: the compere suddenly announced, out of the blue: "I understand there are some members of Her Majesty's Royal Air Force here tonight." I'm ashamed to admit that none of our tiny trio had the nerve to respond – we pretended we just weren't there, looked down at our shoes, and waited for the next victims. He passed on: "Also, I hear, there are some soldiers from Her Majesty's Royal Army" (sic). Not a movement for a few eternal seconds, then, slowly, silently, one solitary soldier in O.G.s (olive greens – soldier's working uniform) stood up, looked round calmly, raised his arms with hands locked in victory salute, turning slowly to left and right. Silence for a tense second or two, then the whole arena erupted into spontaneous and thunderous applause. He sat down. I would dearly love to meet that brave soldier today, and congratulate him for his great bravery in that distant field of "conflict", surely enhanced by our own lack of moral fibre at the time!

Wakiki beach and Diamond Head (postcard)

Soon after, the stars arrived: comedians Bob Hope and Jerry Colonna, and Jayne Mansfield, at the height of her fame. Who came on first? She did, of course, mincing on-stage as best she could in her tight-fitting, flame-red dress, leaving not too much to the imagination. She stopped centre stage, turned sideways, stuck out her chest and waved excitedly to the masses, blonde hair shimmering. For the second time that night, the house erupted: the cheering was indescribable. It was several minutes before Uncle Sam's virile young servicemen would settle down for the show to unfold. I suppose for some, the rest of the show may have been an anti-climax, but it was a most entertaining evening, with belly-laughs galore when Bob Hope and Jerry Colonna formed a double act, bouncing hilarious situations off each-other. How the rest of the show went I have long since forgotten; even so, for us that evening was itself simply unforgettable. For me there had also been a sense of history and of conflict that evening when I remember those pitted barrack blocks from that terrible Japanese attack sixty years ago. We had actually been there that night, and had experienced at first hand, the special atmosphere of Pearl Harbour.

Fledgling Bobby and postcard

Honolulu, despite its plethora of tatty tourist traps, garish souvenir shops, countless bars and other places and sights waiting to be discovered, turned out to be rather an ordinary-looking concrete and power-line-maze sort of place to look at, but behind some of those nondescript, street-side exteriors, there occasionally lurked promises of special things to come. Wandering through unfamiliar streets we suddenly came across what was earthly paradise for we young lads with enforced island-bound celibacy – a strip-tease theatre, with continuous performances. We willingly parted with the few dollars we had left and couldn't wait to take our seats – empty ones at the front, no less! To say we spent a spell-bound hour or two glued to our seats, was an understatement. Tongues hanging out, breathless, unable to take our hungry, organ-stop eyes off those wonderfully gyrating bodies; we sat there transfixed. Aeons later, performances over and back outside, hovering gently over the pavements of Honolulu once again, we wandered aimlessly for a while, hardly believing where we'd just been. When our feet finally did touch the ground, we continued our jaunt around town, a feeling of anti-climax lingering with us for quite a while after.

Hickam Air Force Base December 1957

It was with that feeling of inevitability that we duly reported to R.A.F. Air Movements, Hickam on day three, to return via the reliable but noisy, slow old Dakota DC3 of 1325 "Christmas Airways" Flight. You'd think the Detachment would have given us a few more days for sorting out their filing system, but no chance this time. That first visit of just three days had indeed been crowded with action, experiences and worn-out shoe-leather. Back to Christmas was to return to grim reality, but our brief escape had been worth it and memories were sweet until the next opportunity, should it arise again.

Ranks Pool Hickam Air Force Base

As I have said, one of the occasional perks of working at H.Q. was to be in a good position to learn of any opportunity too good to miss. The next time this happened was another chance to "swan off" to Hawaii – a scheme to give "deserving" cases a welcome break to Oahu, on an official basis. It was called "temporary detachment" and essentially meant that the successful applicant could fly in an official "on duty" capacity – i.e., free, complete with L.O.A. for the duration – for in this instance, a period of three days. Whoever dreamt up this particular, generous scheme I didn't discover, although I could well appreciate there would always be those needy, overstressed, overworked cases on that god-forsaken island who would deserve a spell of leave in "civilisation" as a welcome break. However, for us, it was too good a chance to miss, so before the rules were tightened up, as they were bound to be, we two H.Q. clerks applied and were lucky enough to be among the first groups to go. I must admit, though, that Paddy's was a far more deserving case than mine for this escape from the island – a well-earned rest after a mass of urgent courts-martial typing completed, with a tight deadline. Not long after, the powers that be came to their senses and promptly tightened up the conditions of acceptance, reserving the scheme solely for the most urgent, deserving cases. So, here we were, on our way again, without too many twinges of conscience. Off we flew, friend Paddy from Northern Ireland, and me, hardly believing our luck, albeit only for three short days. We took holiday civvies with us; what we lacked there we could buy, at bargain prices, from the P.X. at Hickam.

At Hickam Air Force Base

Looking somehow smaller than I had imagined, on our gradual approach with decreasing height towards our Oahu landfall, could be seen in turn the other main islands that make up the Hawaiian South Pacific chain: Maui, Hawaii, Molokai – lush, green surrounded by the paling shades of the blue Pacific that shallowed towards their rocky, indented coastlines. On landing, we could see on the runway at Hickam, the M.A.T.S. (Military Air Transport Service) Terminal, line after line of double-decker U.S. Globemaster transport aircraft, with the occasional R.A.F. Hastings squeezed in between, staging through from U.K. to Christmas.

Globemaster ATR Hickam Air Force Base

On Hickam, we were initially dressed in our baggy, creased K.D., comparing very poorly with even the lowest U.S. serviceman in his smartly pressed, well-fitting gabardine. Feeling embarrassingly conspicuous in our own dowdy K.D., we walked our legs off exploring Hickam. We discovered the base laundry with its poetic sign on the door: "Trust Your Duds to Spud's Suds". One shop on the base turned out to be the military tailor's, where we spotted another boastful sign above the front door, which happened to be true, however. We just had to photograph ourselves, in our shabby K.D., under that sign which proudly stated: "Through These Doors Pass the World's Best-Dressed Airmen". Before the picture was taken by a passing U.S. airman, we hurriedly tucked our shirts as tidily as we could into our trousers, brushed our shoes against the back of our legs in true military manner, set our R.A.F. peaked caps straight on our heads, smiled broadly and thought of England. I still have that picture in my album.

Hickam Air Force Base

Hickam tour over, and with ever-better things to discover, we made our way into Honolulu by bus – but what buses! Ordinary service buses, but such floating-on-air transports of delight! Forget the near solid suspension of our U.K. buses back in the mid-fifties, whose hard utility seats were to be endured, and which didn't catch up with those luxurious comfort-wagons we now rode, for many years. These buses' suspensions were as soft as luxury cars. I wondered why such a fantastic difference between ours and theirs?

On the bus into town from Hickam, a landmark that became familiar to us on these journeys, could be seen from miles away – a huge metal pineapple on legs, outside one of the many pineapple canning factories, proclaiming the island's fame for production of this fruit, and its processing industry.

Honolulu wasn't what you would call a beautiful town: practical, busy, lots of downtown concrete and overhead wires, but there was a Woolworths! I wonder how my impressions might change today – 21st century – when tourism and commercialism are so much more developed, no doubt: keeping up with its dual personality as a main base for holiday exploration of the Hawaiian Islands, and at the same time possessing so many attractions of its own within its city limits: International Market, Botanical Gardens, Waikiki;

on to Punchbowl National Cemetery, and Diamond Head, and doubtless many other tourist honey-traps not even thought of during the 1950's.

Royal Hawaiian Hotel - Waikiki

Surfing at Waikiki

With so many places to take in on our three-day leave allocation, how did we manage to fit in most of these during our so-brief stay? Once again, we were lucky, I must admit. We were told to report back to the R.A.F. Detachment Air Movements, Hickam on the third day, to return to Christmas. This we did, only to be told that today's flight was a food-lift with no passenger space available –and come back on day five without fail. Oh, disappointment – another two days in Hawaii! We cheered up as best we could, shouted "Yippee!" when out of range of Air Movements, collected two more days L.O.A. and floated back into Honolulu, and points beyond.

Religiously we turned up again on day five, to be told once again that a food-lift was marginally more important than our return. Another "Yippee", collect two days L.O.A. as you pass Go, and back on day seven or else. Sadly, we couldn't delay our return beyond day seven, so we returned, jubilant that three days had somehow stretched into seven, and not too disappointed – broke but happy!

Diamond Head and Waikiki

Meantime, while we could, we did those tourist spots and continued enjoying our elastic freedom to explore. We took in Waikiki and beach and were impressed by those huge, luxury beach-side hotels (back in the fifties, remember). Best of all, we simply sunbathed on the beach in between our first experience of surf-boarding – largely unsuccessful: unable to ride the surf properly. But at least we had a go and imagined we were like those bronzed Adonises who were making it look easy, out there among the real breakers.

Thieves Market

When collecting our indispensable L.O.A. on day three, we were told about a chance to tour the whole island of Oahu by limousine taxi, if we turned up, in uniform, at the American Forces' Y.M.C.A. in Honolulu, at nine a.m. prompt on the following Sunday morning – tomorrow for us – and all, courtesy of Uncle Sam again.

Y.M.C.A – American Forces

This being too good an opportunity to miss, we made sure we were there on the dot, along with some smartly turned-out American sailors, all in dazzling white. There, waiting to whisk us off round the island, was a small fleet of chrome-gleaming limousine taxis, at a rate that even we could afford! We jumped in, hardly believing our luck, but willing to believe this was really happening to us. The weather was set fair, the driver helpful and a mine of local information, and we were on our way.

International Market at Waikiki

The scenery was spectacular, especially while hugging the south-east coast. Hours later, and timed to perfection, we stopped for lunch at a wonderful Hawaiian restaurant, perched on a cliff-top with superb coastal and ocean views on three sides. We had indeed begun to feel a bit peckish, which helped us enjoy a memorable meal of "Mahi Mahi" – dolphin – without feeling too guilty about what we were eating; helped by its supremely delicious freshness and a most piquant pink sauce to go with it, that I'd never before, or since, tasted the like. I'll swear I can still savour that sauce even now, when I think of it.

We were now turning inland to take in the interior of Oahu. Here the rugged coastal scenery gave way to more open, rolling vistas of undulating land, with distant volcanic ridges lurking ahead towards the heart of the island. Soon, dotted everywhere on both sides, were mile after mile of low, spiky bushes, as far as the eye could see: pineapples – for which Hawaii is justly famous.

Botanical gardens Hawaii

Curios – International Market Place

Waikiki Hotel

Minutes later, in the distance, we could make out a small, lonely shack, which turned out to be an open-fronted cabin. As we drew nearer, we could see that it was filled with several huge, tall fridges. This was luckily our next stop; we found these appliances to be brim-filled with freshly-cut fruit – trimmed, cored, cut, sliced, diced, ringed, pulped – you name it – pineapple. I cannot accurately describe the taste of these oh-so-fresh fruits – nothing like the tinned variety, or even the whole ones you can buy at the supermarket today. "Fresh" didn't do it justice – the nearest I can come to describing the indescribable was "pepperminty-superfresh".

We ate our fill of this ambrosia, then on inland we continued, until we came to the volcanic heart of the island, steeply eroded lava ravines, now lush and tree-covered, radiating from clouded volcanic peaks like the spokes of a gigantic, irregular cartwheel. The roadside where we stopped to take in the impressive vista viewpoint, stared almost sheer down into V-shaped gorges, forested and begging for yet another bout of photography. Then our eyes were led upwards to the jagged peaks that seemed to loom right over us on either side – we couldn't take our eyes off those majestic summits.

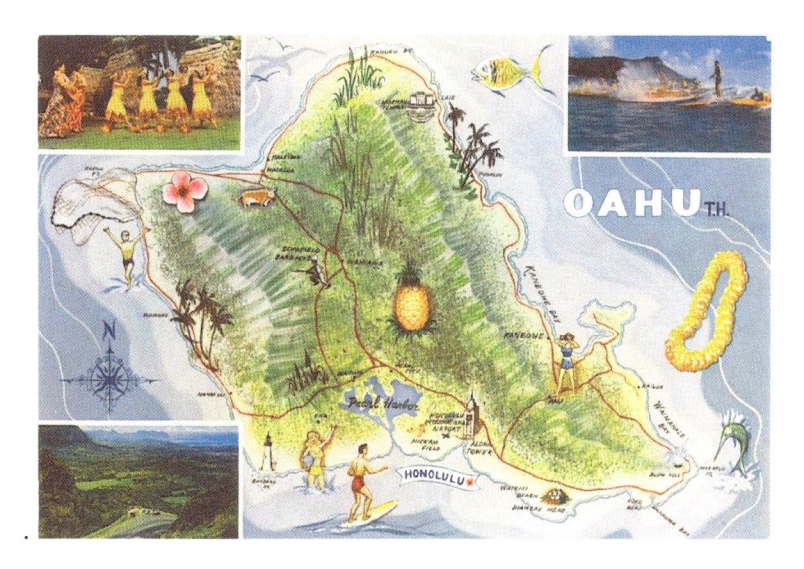

Oahu postcard

In the very heart of the island, we passed by the massive Schofield Army Barracks, famous for locations in such cinema greats as "From Here to Eternity". Later we toured the huge, extensive Mormon temple in a rather remote spot tucked away in the north-east of the island – with features unlike any other traditional place of worship I'd ever seen – pretentious, ornamental pools, fringed with white columns descending the hillside with stepped waterfalls and neat, dead-straight avenues of travellers' palms.

Mormon Temple

I guessed they could afford all that impressive ostentation – an intentional way of making a statement of their religious wealth.

The rest of the day passed as it had already progressed – a fantastic exploration of an island setting such as I had ever seen before – a truly once-in-a-lifetime experience. However, as far as our island tour was concerned, it wasn't quite over yet. We had seen the large-scale, impressive sights; now the scale lessened, but still the impact was sustained. An insignificant-looking pool by the roadside where we stopped on the way back to Honolulu turned out to be a bottomless pit – I took the driver's word for this piece of information and didn't dive in to test his claim. Evidently, this flooded hole in the ground was connected to the sea a few miles away, once again all very volcanic.

Black sands Hawaii

Back on the outskirts of modern Honolulu, but years ago standing in quiet solitude on the hillside above the old town, was a little Anglican church of grey volcanic stone, centrepiece of the graveyard for Hawaii's former kings and queens, sealed away in time in carefully kept underground vaults, with worn steps leading down to mysterious, locked doorways. Impressive names and titles of more local monarchs were inscribed on large table-graves in between. A small green and grey oasis of peace and calm amid the surrounding bustle of today's busy Honolulu. To sum up the day's tour: one impressive, unforgettable Sunday.

Waikiki beach

The next day – our last – and still fired with the spirit to explore while we could, we wandered up the Honolulu main street that led to Waikiki Beach. Before crossing to the ocean-side, we discovered the International Market – a maze of tortuous paths that meandered through an endless variety of tourist-oriented local craft and souvenir shops and stalls, amid shady trees. Many different artefacts were being hand-crafted on the spot by local sun-burnt Hawaiians, all exactly like I imagined Ernest Hemingway to have looked. They must have been making a small fortune – its location just across the road from those rows of luxurious up-market hotels and restaurants that opened on to Waikiki Beach – would have ensured this.

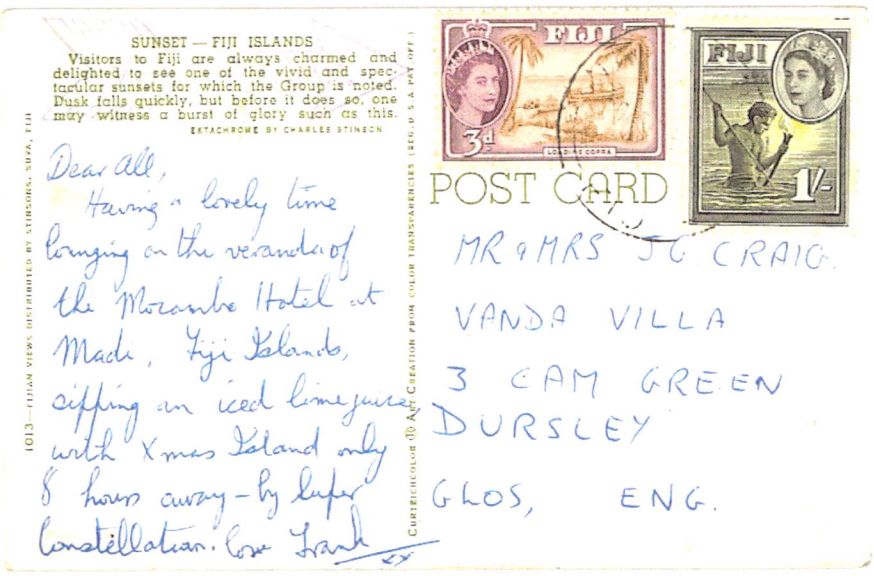

SUNSET — FIJI ISLANDS
Visitors to Fiji are always charmed and delighted to see one of the vivid and spectacular sunsets for which the Group is noted. Dusk falls quickly, but before it does so, one may witness a burst of glory such as this.
EKTACHROME BY CHARLES STINSON

Dear All,
 Having a lovely time lounging on the veranda of the Mocambo Hotel at Nadi, Fiji Islands, sipping an iced lime juice, with Xmas Island only 8 hours away — by Super Constellation. Love Frank

POST CARD

MR & MRS J G CRAIG.
VANDA VILLA
3 CAM GREEN
DURSLEY
GLOS,   ENG.

Bird of Paradise and Hawaiian sunset

Later, we visited the Botanical Gardens – not everyone's cup of tea, but I would guarantee that, once inside, you couldn't fail to be captivated by the wonderful display of flowers, shrubs, bushes and magnificent trees, each in their own natural setting, the whole gardens a peaceful haven of green with vivid splashes of flowering colour: from the smallest orchids, through many varieties of national emblem hibiscus, brightly blooming bushes and shrubs, to an endless variety of trees, each with their own flowers, fruits and seeds. I remember especially, the canon-ball trees, whose ripening red fruits would suddenly disperse with an audible report; grey, multi-limbed banyan trees, whose masses of arterial roots fell straight down from their branches, disappearing underground; and trees whose long, curved seedpods hung down like black, drooping, over-ripe bananas.

Fern Forests, Hawaii

Cramming in yet another spectacular location, we next made our way up beyond Waikiki, to the Punchbowl U.S. National War Cemetery, where collective American pride and sorrow, in remembering its thousands of servicemen lost in the Pacific theatre of World War II, was eloquently demonstrated in endless row upon row of small, grey stone plaques, stretching away across the wide, shallow valley in a sea of neat, short grass, almost as far as the eye could see. Studded in precise mathematical lines curving away across this huge volcanic depression – down one side and up the other – this was Punchbowl. Flanked on either side by lush volcanic ridges, to the east by the ever-impressive Diamond Head, stretching down to the sea to the water-side hotels of Waikiki and on, into Honolulu itself. All this and more could be taken in from our breath-taking viewpoint, high on the cemetery's western corner.

Always popular with the lads back on Christmas, were the pin-up magazines and soft-porn sex-books of the day, freely available at every bookstand in Honolulu; also, the usual novelties – tastefully-illustrated playing-cards, joke toys and the like. We brought back what we could afford between us. My contribution was a book I had spotted and bought, full of bawdy humour – jokes, cartoons, suggestive articles, studded with the usual double-entendres – and called, appropriately, "Over Sexteen". It soon disappeared after I got back. I lent it to someone, who lent it to a friend, passing from hand to hand, tent to tent: it just didn't come back.

I wonder now how we managed to crowd all these experiences into just under seven days leave? I suppose the pace of life, our youthful energy, together with a burning desire for a unique chance to see what, in all probability, would never come our way again, coupled with the progressive good luck of an extending period of leave – three to seven days – from our Christmas home-base – all factors that contributed to that short, week-long spree.

Finally, to claim a third visit to Oahu is, I must admit, stretching the truth a little. This time I was at last on my way home to U.K. at the end of my Christmas Island stint, stopping, at Hickam Air Base, to let our old Hastings aircraft refuel, with time only for a hurried transit mess meal before flying on homeward via San Francisco, more of which later. However, I made it count as visit number three.

Such was our mid-Pacific isolation, Rarotonga somehow figured in the list of temporary island escapes, as a Dakota staging stop for refuelling or running repairs. Some of our food was flown in from Australia – a Hastings aircraft would be used for the regular run. Occasionally there was some spare capacity on these flights, and the crews would let a few "deserving" cases share the trip. A Rarotonga Island stop-over would sometimes even occur en route, especially if an aircraft went u/s (unserviceable) somewhere on the run. One day a young airman friend of Allan the barber found himself in such a happy situation and at this particular time, met and fell in love with a local Rarotongan girl while stranded there. Understandably upset when faced with the looming prospect of his return to U.K., could he or should he stay and marry her or not? We never did learn the outcome of this rather poignant situation, with the vast and real separation of thousands of miles of Pacific Ocean.

Catamarans (for hotel guests) postcard

POETRY!

"Poetry" could be "created" in a number of ways: when the need to rebel against ongoing conditions needed to find expression; or if sudden inspiration triggered the flashing light-bulb of some creative urge; perhaps merely for a joke; or even with no specific reason at all, other than relieve the boredom of the slow passage of time: if the fit took you, the words could flow, never mind the literary quality or rhyming metre; you just had to get it off your chest and on to paper. Once composed and re-worked to your satisfaction, it would be typed out, duplicated on an ancient, temperamental Banda or Gestetner machine (they always seemed to break down at the worst moment) under cover at work, passed around among friends, and as often as not, worn out with passage from hand to sweaty hand, forgotten when the novelty passed, or occasionally filed carefully away with other island possessions. Usually humorous but ever straight from the heart, they were always based on those difficult, shared, personal experiences.

My own creation was forgotten – I failed to keep a surviving copy – for almost fifty years, until it re-surfaced when my friend Allan the barber recently re-discovered it among his long-unsorted Christmas Island papers and, not suspecting its authorship, showed it to me recently, along with other newly-sorted memorabilia. I looked at the poem's subscription: F.J.C. Anon. 1957 and suddenly realised this was how I usually identified my scribblings. I re-read it, more closely; the memory-banks gradually cleared and I remembered writing it. It had certainly been heart-felt, although light-heartedly Utopian. Here it is:

No Wine Women or Song (Just Sand)

Last night as I stirred restlessly,

On my safari bed,

The damned thing tipped up sideways,

And I landed on my head.

The tent blurred out of focus,

A flash lit up the night,

I felt my senses reeling,

And I flaked out like a light.

As I transcended nothingness,

I stopped to look a while

When suddenly I spied afar

A golden coral isle.

I floated a little closer

To get a closer view,

And to my great amazement

T'was an island that I knew.

Christmas Island floated gently

A jewel in an azure sea,

I walked between the palm groves

Which grew luxuriantly.

It must have been reveille

For a tannoy message said,

"It's half past nine, my dearies,

Time you weren't in bed.

You'll miss your lovely breakfast,

Eggs, bacon, bangers and toast,

With a plateful of Rice Crispies,

On the fruit you love the most."

Work starts at ten-thirty onwards,

At twelve they serve you lunch,

The rank-men wait upon you –

The officers serve you punch.

There's no set time for knock-off,

Just three o'clock or four,

You lounge all day on your backside,

You don't work any more.

The very last H-bomb was dropped

Ten years ago today.

I think that they've forgotten us

At Grapple "X" U.K.

They domesticated land-crabs

To do the washing up,

They draw new claws from Unit Stores

They've never dropped a cup.

The reef disintegrated,

Last April or July,

All sharks, too, have gone away,

But no-one knows quite why.

There is no rainy season,

To dampen anyone,

That's not the only reason,

That nothing's ever done.

Each man has a female servant,

Just like young Jayne Mansfield,

You don't have to wed, for a double bed,

The dark night's lips are sealed.

There's no such thing as bull-night

Nobody cares a cus

The old girls do all that has to be done,

Which seems quite right to us.

There's no such thing as pay here,

The NAAFI's always free,

The Gift Shop is just what it says

It's paradise for me.

Wait – everything is fading,

I hear somebody speak –

"Get up, you lazy bastard,

You're on earlies all this week."

F.J.C. Anon. 1957

We even composed our own Christmas Island National Anthem – more widely circulated I'd say, than other occasional verse. Again, not what you could call of high literary merit, but again which certainly expressed in so many words, the conditions in which we often found ourselves, and their effect upon us. I wonder if it was ever set to music? Here goes:

The Christmas Island National Anthem

O, we are the Megaton Warriors,

Decked out in our K.D. and sweat,

We live on a tropical island,

Which we'd all like to forget.

And when we get back to old England,

And step on our Motherland's shore,

We'll burn all our Khaki to ashes,

And never leave Blighty no more.

Out here we've got land-crabs and bedbugs,

And rats that run over our beds,

Our feet bloom with lovely green fungus,

The sun, it goes straight to our heads,

Our tents are like sieves when it's raining,

You get a cold shower in bed,

If it wasn't for mail from our girlfriends,

We think we'd be better off dead.

A petrol can holds all our water,

For washing and drinking and shaves,

And under the sand it's all coral,

We can't even dig our own graves,

So they feed us, to keep us from dying,

On corned beef and pom, and cold tea,

When they say we've enough, then they're lying,

What would hardly feed one, must feed three.

We're all going home very shortly,

Or at least that is what they all say,

It might be a week or a fortnight,

Or even six months yesterday,

But when our time comes, we'll be happy,

We'll all dance the hula with glee,

Shouting "Stick all your tropical islands,

It's Blighty, dear old Blighty for me."

Another poem of troubled dream sequences I made up, expressed unhappier aspects of island life, recalled nine years after my return; was it, I wondered, a case of looking back in anger, or just a necessary piece of English Literature homework required by my first-year teacher training tutor?

La Reve Passe

When deep within the land of nod the same dream keeps returning,

To shake me by the jugular and set my throat a-burning;

That scorching, parching sun's so hot it drives me round the bend,

Oh, why the hell can't I wake up – when will the damned thing end?

I'm back in Christmas Island where, in celibacy steep'd

I'm whiling 'way my one-year tour on this small atoll heap'd

With whitest coral sand; inland the sleepy blue lagoon

A haven where mad Englishmen at noonday often swoon

Beneath the tall and gently swaying palms, to share their slab

With Christmas Island fauna like the hoary old land-crab –

A bold crustacean versed well in the art of self-defence,

And also quite a dab-hand at the side-step shuffle, hence

Its great demand at dances, mess-nights, NAAFI clubs and such.

One timely warning, keep well clear of its hydraulic clutch,

(Used here in workshops as a wrench for bending iron bars,

And in the airmen's mess, it seemed, for prising open jars.)

Jerboas that played here at night (we had no micing cats),

Were "harmless, chaps" to M.O.D. – to us were simply rats

That scraped and sped across our unadorned, recumbent forms;

In ragged tents, oblivious of rain and tropic storms.

What brought me here with countless other military slaves?

Back in the days when Britain thought that she still ruled the waves,

The P.M. and his mongers, with some Aldermaston ones,

All thought they'd have a go exploding lots of megatons,

Way out in mid-Pacific, out of everybody's way;

And let's all have the biggest bang on Guy Fawkes' next birthday!

The big day came – and went – alas the clouds were in the way!

The boffins in their fall-out shelters wouldn't see that day,

The full potentialities of man's destructive force.

But what the hell, we'll try again tomorrow, yes, of course!

The mushroom rose, the wild birds died, the graceful palm-trees charred.

We, crouching low a few short miles away, were praying hard.

The heat was great upon our backs, the shockwaves felled us there,

But glory be, we're still alive, not grilled a medium rare.

Life on this far-off coral isle left much to be desired:

A year was much too long to stay before one's tour expired.

Not many weeks elapsed before small worries magnified,

Until unbalance led to contemplating suicide.

The hidden reef with jagged teeth invited those past care,

To wade and face its cruel embrace, to end it all right there.

I well remember standing guard on one who'd been pulled back,

In troubled sleep, and I in troubled wakefulness before.

His reason? Mum forgot her weekly letter once – no more.

How could we cool perspiring bodies 'neath the salty waves,

While just beyond the golden beach the waiting coral paves

The way to jagged death; while off inland in blue lagoons,

(As salty as a Scotsman's porage) lurked most afternoons,

The yellow-bellied sand-sharks, rip-tide currents, manta rays:

As good a place as any here for one to end one's days!

Although "issued" in jest, there were certainly important "messages" in my final missive – sent in advance of repatriation to the homes of loved ones by those about to return to U.K., all inevitably in questionable condition after a year on the island. Once again, between the lines could be seen those less than salubrious experiences that would certainly need a period of re-adjustment on return to civilisation.

Notice of Return

ISSUED IN SOLEMN WARNING [THIS DAY], 1957/8

To the neighbours, friends and relatives of ………………………………...

Lock your daughters in their rooms.

Fill the icebox with cold canned beer and get those civvies out of mothballs.

Very soon the above mentioned will once more be in your midst, dehydrated.

And demoralised to take his place once again as a human being with freedom, and justice for all engaged in life, liberty and the somewhat delayed pursuit of happiness. In making your joyous preparations to welcome him back into organised society, you must make allowances for the crude and miserable environment which has been his lot for ……. months.

In a word, he must be treated with "CAUTION". He might be a trifle Polynesian, suffering from Crabitis or a little too much Toddy.

Therefore, show no alarm if he prefers to sit on the floor instead of on a chair, always kicks his boots against the front door before entering the house, or that he has a tendency to salute anyone of importance.

His diet should consist mainly of dehydrated potato with small quantities of dried peas or other tinned vegetables. Fresh food, especially milk, should be avoided for the first two weeks and then introduced into his diet gradually. His language may be rather embarrassing at first but, in a relatively short time he can be taught to speak plain English again. Never ask him why the boy down the street had a higher rank than he, and make no flattering remarks about the Army or R.A.F. in his presence.

For the first few months (until he has been housebroken) be especially watchful when he is in the company of women, particularly young and beautiful specimens. After seeing beautiful women being wooed by handsome men in the movies, he thinks he is master of the art himself.

His intentions will be sincere, even though dishonourable. Keep in mind, that beneath his tanned and rugged exterior there beats a heart of GOLD. Treasure this, it will be the only thing of value he has left. Treat him with kindness, tolerance and occasional quarts of good liquor, and you will be able to rehabilitate that which is the hollow shell of the happy and youthful man you once knew.

(signed) B. READY

Officer i/c Rehabilitation Advisory Committee.

THE BOMB

Why were we all here, on the island in the first place? A frightening combination of international politics, a mad race for nuclear supremacy in a current cold war situation, that many hoped would prevent global nuclear war; space in the middle of the world's largest ocean to experiment with their growing, increasingly powerful atomic and hydrogen bombs: nuclear weapons of mass destruction capability; but most of all, in my opinion, a successful ploy to prevent me from realising one of my three original overseas choices.

The particular operation at which I was present was "Grapple", divided into Phases X, Y and Z. To detonate one single bomb, a staggering number of supporting servicemen from all three of the Armed Services – mainly R.A.F. – were needed; plus civilian scientific teams. So, there was I, a very small clerical cog in a very large nuclear wheel, waiting and wondering what would happen, stuck on this remote island in quite primitive conditions.

8th November 1957 – Plane Overhead

In some ways we were early guinea-pigs – always hotly denied by successive governments – where the potential hazards were not fully known or appreciated; nor was time made to establish contamination limits or necessary effective precautions. There were always rumours and tales about radio-active contamination, mysterious diseases, bleak future life prospects; whether we were too close to ground zero on detonation; suspicion or rejection by wives or partners, via the frightening prospect of a "Dear John" letter, worried about passing on of long-term effects of radioactivity to children, and other factors that remained unexplained, ignored or in ignorance of. (All these have unfortunately been sadly realised in the years since, by far too many of those involved).

We prepared in our various ways, for our first big bang – Grapple X – which was due to be detonated on 5th November 1957, poetically. Little was known about what exactly happens when a device of this magnitude goes off; they say that ignorance is bliss, but not after this event. All information was on a "need- to-know" basis (i.e., normal security) which meant that our level we were told nothing we didn't need to know, including, obviously, necessary basic precautions.

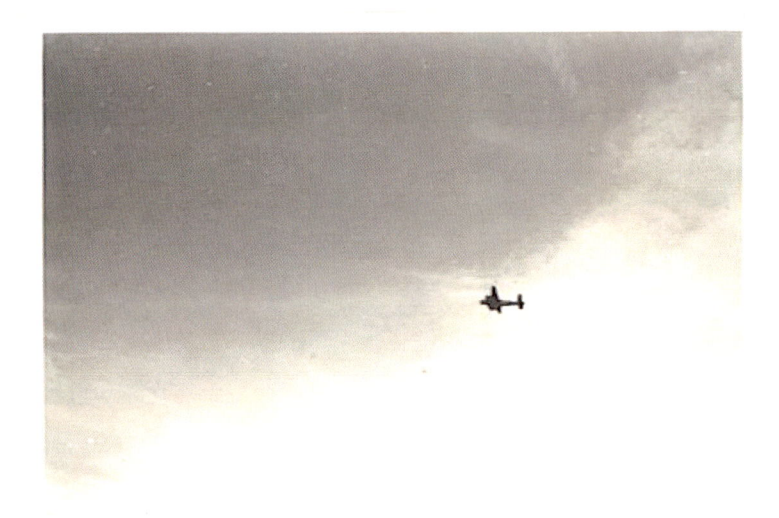

206 Squadron Shackleton Reece (Grapple X)

Prior to the bomb drop we had to undertake various "dry run" procedures, including emergency evacuation – what to do if the bomb-carrying Valiant crashed on take-off with its armed load on board. In that case it was evacuation by three-ton lorry to Port London. Each group of us was allocated a specific numbered lorry on which we had to carry out embarking procedure on this particular day. Our lorry, including officers as well as other ranks, unknown to us, had been recently employed on emptying the chemical toilets and disposing of the waste in 45-gallon drums, to the island's "shit farm" (sewage disposal facility), but it had not been too carefully checked for cleaning afterwards and before our not so "dry" run that day, carrying that unmistakable ambience of human effluent. This resulted in our mixed group of evacuees having to climb aboard a much less than sanitised vehicle (to put it nicely), for which the offending cleansing squad were charged and punished. We wondered afterwards if the witch-hunt would have been as rigorous had only lower ranks had to use that particular lorry that day – or am I being too cynical?

The due day came and passed – the weather wasn't exactly right, and so on until the 8th. That morning, early, we were all herded towards a coconut plantation well away from the Main Camp and told to enter the grove – for some kind of protection, we weren't yet sure exactly what kind. We then had to squat on our heels, facing away from ground zero – at least we were told that much – close our eyes tightly, cover our eyes with our hands, and tuck our heads between our knees, but only for the flash and heat. As soon as these had passed, we were to leave our shelter at a run, before some kind of blast – the shock-waves – might dislodge coconuts from the "sheltering" palms, on to our unprotected heads! You must appreciate that we had no protective clothing, dressed only in our everyday K.D. – short-sleeved shirts and long trousers. We crouched and waited. First came the flash, which, even in our fully averted positions, was just like a camera flash going off in front of our eyes. Many of my friends told me afterwards that they even saw the bones of their fingers and hands before their tight-shut eyes during the flash – like a momentary x-ray. I don't recall this happening myself, but it could have been something I didn't specially remember after the event. I keep an open mind. The heat – a few long seconds after the flash – was like a hot oven door being opened against my back; it felt as though it went all the way through my body at the time. Time to run! We dashed smartly from our tree-cover, away from any risk from shockwave, gravity-fed coconut showers upon our vulnerable heads, and simply stood around in loose groups in the open, like so many spare parts, wondering what would happen next – we had been told no more. Seconds later, we rather forcibly found out! An indeterminate pause, and several of what I can only describe as loud thuds reached us – the shockwaves. All around me I saw people falling over; I somehow managed to keep my feet (was this what hammer-throwing does for your nuclear survival, I thought later?) Then we all saw that most awesome, orange-glowing mushroom cloud spawning in the sky – with shades of yellow, mauve and red –writhing and swelling upwards like one rampant, out-of-control tumour, the high surrounding cloud simply melting away like an invisible halo ahead of the fearsome, roiling vortex: a truly unforgettable sight. How do you describe the indescribable?

Bomb Test – ^{8th} November 1957

When the officers in charge finally gathered themselves and us together, they herded us back to Main Camp, with tangible feelings of anti-climax. We continually looked back at that huge, now fully-grown mushroom, now comprising several layers, like a block of fantasy high-rise flats from outer space. Later, we saw the R.A.F. Valiant bomber returning from its lethal drop; later still the photoreconnaissance and "sniffer" Canberras and finally, hours later, the ocean-sweeping Shackletons.

I think we had the rest of the day off, perhaps to contemplate the implications of the morning's events, each at his own private level; also, to frequently steal glances towards the gradually dispersing mushroom cloud – still a huge, awesome sight – tall but spreading outwards – now a more misty-grey, gradually dissipating and merging with the higher, regathering clouds of the atmosphere.

Valiant returning after dropping the bomb

The blast that had felled most of us also caused much other damage, much of which we never learned about at the time. One incident we did witness during these moments, was the sight of a five-gallon tea urn flying past, narrowly missing us. Back at Main Camp we found a number of tents demolished; the whole atmosphere here was eerie for days after the detonation, a state that lasted much longer than the mushroom cloud, which gradually dispersed later that day, as atmospheric conditions returned to some normality.

If you thought too much about the day's events, who could fail to feel a sense of impending doom – that all this testing was definitely not "right". Time may since have healed some thoughts and fears with their passing, I guess, but they were very real and close at the time; not all have been consigned to the deepest recesses of our memories, however. We need no reminding, with each premature passing of a friend and contemporary, or of enduring chronic conditions of others – these are the real prompts.

Having realised what should have been obvious from the beginning – that we needed better protective clothing and safer procedures, for the next drop at which I was present, Grapple "Y", in April 1958, we were better prepared, although we still had no idea how close we were to ground zero. White overall dungarees, white balaclavas, sunglasses, white gauntlet gloves and stout shoes were the order of the day. These we called "zoot suits"; we had great pleasure in taking each other's photographs adorned with this nuclear fancy-dress, in appropriate and inappropriate poses. When the test day arrived, we simply had to lay face-down, full-length on the ground until everything this even bigger bomb could throw at us had passed over. Good job, I thought, that it hadn't been raining beforehand, the way it often did. The now-familiar mushroom cloud again appeared and grew, if anything more awesome than the last. Some time after the event, we were generously given a small black and white "official" photograph of the mushroom cloud, which I have to this day, along with some of my own, stuck into my ancient but treasured island photo album, and the rest of the visual record of my year on the island.

Before I could witness the third and final phase of Operation Grapple – Grapple "Z" – I was repatriated to the U.K., a veteran of almost a year on Christmas Island. The dangers, however, were not finally over until we touched down at R.A.F. Lyneham, as I will explain.

As a minor postscript, after the detonations and before we returned home, some of us who still had some misplaced Grapple enthusiasm, decorated our kitbags with colourful Grapple crests – a cormorant with a four-pronged grappling hook clutched in its claws, representing the four Armed Services. I still have mine in the loft upstairs.

A view of the beach and main camp from the air

HOMECOMING AND AFTER

GETTING BACK

Finally, it seemed that incredibly, one moment I was almost getting to like the island – a seasoned inhabitant of eleven whole months standing – and the next, told I was to be on my way home within days. We were even having bets on who in our Section would be the first to go. Of course I was longing to be back – couldn't wait to be shot of the heat, working, eating and living conditions – ragged, stuffy old tents, sand everywhere, the heat and sweat, food that left so much to be desired, side-stepping land-crabs everywhere, working life in temporary buildings in much less than ideal conditions and levels of acceptability way below what should have been: in a word – primitive. But in some ways, was the place almost growing on me? Was there a chance that, here and there, I'd be almost sorry to leave this desert island? Yes, underneath all the happy anticipation of return to civilisation and "normality", there were aspects of this place I'd miss, even if I didn't realise it at the time.

Land crab

The climate, the wild but peaceful, beckoning interior of the island with its unique flora and fauna; good friends to have to leave; even some of the less pleasant features I'd got used to and which didn't seem so unbearable any more: had I become too tolerant of these? Time to stifle all these feelings and concentrate on my approaching return. Good-byes to good friends, kitbags packed and re-packed: can I cram everything I had accumulated and acquired, not lost or broken? Any remaining consumables and "essentials" sent from home by well-meaning relatives, especially ever-concerned mothers and wives; prized possessions and souvenirs, official kit items including full U.K. blues, and all the rest that always seems that must go into kitbags. So, we are still in tropical K.D. for at least the time being. (a small point, but to be relevant later on my return journey). Longing at last became reality via the flight home. Our return transport of delight for us, was the old, noisy R.A.F. Hastings with its four piston engines, but also, as it fortunately turned out a short while later, reliable and flexible. At least we were pointed in the right direction. Did time fly by or pass agonisingly slowly before leaving? I can't remember clearly: too many mixed emotions at the time: most likely a bit of each, depending on what was happening at the time.

The first leg of the return flight was almost pleasant – an all-too-brief refuelling stop at Oahu, Hawaii, for both aircraft and passengers; but no time to slip away from Hickam, but at least a first brief respite from old lady Hastings. No more Waikiki, Honolulu, Diamond Head or island tours, or luckily, enough time to miss them before we sardines were re-canned, sealed aboard and on our way again: over the Eastern Pacific towards West Coast U.S.A. and Travis Air Base, San Francisco. Unfortunately, again, no time here either, for even an hour or so on the town for a brief Cooks tour, so on we rattled, over the spectacular, snow-patched Rocky Mountains – brown-grey and grey-brown – far below.

The Rockies

On then to Offut Air Base, Omaha, Nebraska, our next, mid-western pit-stop. Here, luckily, we were given the day for an all-too-short furlough to Omaha city, of which, needless to say, we all took advantage.

My main memories here firstly, were of, at lunchtime, a king-size steak – "T-bone a la Hasty Tasty", generously overhanging both sides of my oval plate. After all, this was mid-west cattle country, to satisfy those generous American appetites.

On the way home via U.S.A.

Omaha at night

Later, as evening wore on, we became mesmerised by the glittering array (to us, after a year shut away minus most of life's little luxuries) of the high-class consumer products on offer to Mr and Mrs Omaha, via an endless twisting tangle of multi-coloured neon, garishly showing off such things as giant four-poster beds, with gauzy muslin wraps floating behind huge plate-glass windows, and exclusive, frothy wedding dresses; these particular images stand out in my memory. Also, indelibly printed on my homeward-bound mind, lines of closely-parked American cars, neatly and closely packed like rectangular steers, within metred parking bays, corralled up and down the main streets – something I'd not seen before; all these cowering under more miles of indecently throbbing neon.

Badlands, Nebraska (postcard)

Then all too soon it was back aboard the Hastings for another lengthy leg, this time north-eastwards towards Labrador, Northern Canada. Now, although it was summertime, believe me, when we climbed down from the aircraft on to that Northern Canadian concrete at Goose Bay Air Base, still only wearing our tropical K.D., boy, was it cold – absolute brass-monkey weather! We complained and were grudgingly allowed to change into our U.K. blues – warmer admittedly but still inadequate in that far-northern chill, until we clambered aboard the Hastings again and took off.

Mississippi – U.S.A

This time it was definitely home next stop at last. However, fate must have been quietly waiting for us to slip into a spirit of false optimism. Somewhere over the North Atlantic, after we had passed the point of no return from Goose Bay, those of us peering through the windows could now and then make out tiny dots of white far below, against the dull, grey ocean – icebergs! Just then, the captain's voice came over the tannoy: one of our four engines had stopped – and, yes, we could see that miscreant propeller turning slowly in the headwind, with those tiny icebergs still far below us. We duly went through full ditching procedure: May Wests on; here's the oxygen; this is how you crouch and prepare for the worst. I remember, the only thing I was worried about at that moment, was not the prospect of doing an aerial Titanic, but the possibility that my camera, Christmas Island slides and photographs might be lost.

The captain, bless his optimistic soul, decided that, in his estimation, he could make it at least to R.A.F. Aldergrove, Northern Ireland, to which we diverted. Mae West lifejackets and oxygen masks re-stowed, some atmosphere of calm slowly returned. Hours later, when we eventually neared the Irish coast, the captain, ever positive, decided we could make it to our original destination of Lyneham after all, much to our collective relief. But fate was at it again. While crossing the Irish Sea, a second engine failed.

However, being British, we duly stiffened our upper lips, putting our joint faiths in our Captain, that he would, of course, deliver us safe and in one piece, to Lyneham. Wasn't this his job – his sole aim in life, and this aircraft was designed to keep flying on only two engines, wasn't it?

As if that wasn't enough, however, on our final approach to the airfield, a third engine feathered (turned at reduced power), so our laden plane landed on one and a half engines out of four. The collective sigh of relief from inside that Hastings could be heard, I'm sure, in the Lyneham control tower at that moment.

The final insult, however, was still to come: we hadn't even enough power left to taxi unaided to our disembarkation bay. We were frustratingly forced to wait for what seemed like hours until a tractor arrived to where we were stranded like a beached whale some way up the runway, to tow us ignominiously in. While awaiting its arrival, the main door was opened, for fresh air and relief; some of us couldn't resist jumping down to the ground to make sure we'd really made it, and to touch the first lush, green English grass we'd seen for a year. Funny the things we had missed.

The rest was anti-climax. We were duly disembarked, processed through Lyneham, and hurried on to Swindon railway station for our various home destinations, after farewells to good friends made on the island; and that was it.

Read the notice

I later heard that the pilot of the Hastings was decorated for his skilful handling of the aircraft: ensuring our return from what we had sometimes compared with Alcatraz. As far as I was concerned, he deserved the Victoria Cross!

We had at the time, of course, no real idea of the perilous conditions we had been in that day – how close to a cold, watery end in the Atlantic, or on our final approach to that Wiltshire airfield. Much later, in retrospect maybe, having had time to reflect on what could have been, the possibilities would have presented themselves to us much more forcibly than then. But, what the hell – compared with events and conditions – real and potential – endured and come through relatively unscathed over the past year on that mid-Pacific nuclear test-bed; with excited minds crammed with anticipation of homecoming pleasures and civilisation, what further damage could this last-minute hitch do to us? Who would argue with the old adage of ignorance being bliss in this case?

HOMECOMING

A summer homecoming was some compensation for the sudden deterioration in weather quality from what I had become used to on my tropical island "home" over the past year. To improve matters further, I was back in my wonderful Gloucestershire countryside in its state, to quote Laurie Lee, of "leafy levitation". Climate and exotic location apart, there was simply no comparison between these two places, at any time of year, but especially now in high summer, and two months leave before my next U.K. posting. Without it fully sinking in first of all, I was also back to those little taken-for-granted comforts that we don't always appreciate until we are suddenly having to go without them: full mobility, more quality leisure time, freedom to go where and when you wish, in my case, jumping on my motorbike and driving where the whim took me. I could enjoy good home cooking, eat out in style, meet old local friends for a drink and chat; the list was almost endless, and I was enjoying gradually catching up with them one by one, savouring with all five senses, each improvement in lifestyle, so lacking on the island. My dad had thoughtfully and lovingly kept my old motorbike in good running order for me during my absence, but of course, as soon as I'd been on it again for a few days, I wanted something bigger and faster. We duly motored up to Gloucester on my old B.S.A. 250, swapped it and drove home again the proud owner of a new beige B.S.A. 650cc Gold Flash, and the country was mine again!

As I have already mentioned, my mother was busy feeding up her undernourished son, and I soon put on more weight than was probably good for me, but all in a good cause. I quickly forgot the sad lack of quality and quantity in the Christmas diet that I'd almost become used to and revelled in the variety of my new daily calories. If I had to admit it, I was to a degree back to my war-time childhood eating habits – fry-ups, buns for tea, buttered pikelets, toasted to near-charcoal perfection, but definitely no mashed potato until I lost that unhappy association with that dreaded dehydrated ooze, "pom" we had been recently forced to eat on Christmas.

My U.K. posting turned out to be to the R.A.F. Record Office, Gloucester, just thirteen miles from my home, twenty minutes down the A38 on my Gold Flash. Home then, was a regular weekend port of call when not socialising with new R.A.F. mates on camp at Barnwood and Innsworth – until I met and married the girl of my dreams and went overseas again.

Ironically, my job at Record Office was overseas postings. Although my own clerical trade-group wasn't included in my job remit, my mate in the next office was, and in less than three years I was on P.W.R. again, with those same three choices to make on my overseas warning form. This time, being to an extent "on the inside", all three location choices did become reality during my next overseas tour. My friend first asked me if I'd like to go to Singapore, the likeliest posting of my three old choices. Yes, please! When he knew my draft number, he asked me if I'd like to go to sail out on the very last troopship run to the Far East, aboard S.S. Nevasa. Yes, please again! We embarked from Southampton one misty April morning in 1961. We called at Gibraltar, Malta, Suez, Aden, Negombo (Sri Lanka), on the way to Singapore, not only stopping to visit all these places en route, but gradually becoming acclimatised to the Far Eastern heat over the period of our three-week "cruise". Most of the Nevasa's military passengers comprised an amalgamation of two old Scottish Highland Regiments into the newly formed Queen's Own Highlanders, posted en masse to Singapore. There certainly was hilarity at every port of call, when these lads were let loose at each location, leading each time on their return on board in varying degrees of inebriation, to confinement to the ship's cells.

I spent a most enjoyable three years in Singapore, during which time I went on leave to Hong Kong, shown around by an old friend from Record Office; so each of my original three choices was eventually realised, however briefly. I travelled through Malaya and Thailand; during a holiday well and truly away from it all in the central Malayan jungle, I was to renew my acquaintance with a more deadly relative of my old friends the Christmas Island mosquitos, and was bitten by a malarial cousin. Fortunately, it turned out to be the benign, non-recurring type. I recovered after near-fatal high temperature admission to the British Military Hospital, Singapore, and have never been troubled by it since. Incidentally, I could have stayed in the B.M.H. for longer had I felt so inclined, as the medical officers there had never before had a serviceman catch malaria in that particular part of Malaya and wanted to use me as a twice-daily blood-test guinea-pig. However, my wife and a busy athletics season were calling me much more strongly, and I eventually managed to discharge myself – as much as a serviceman was able to do so in a military hospital – away from the clutches of those blood-testing medico-vampires.

I was to meet up again eight years later with the sergeant P.T.I. who found a hammer for me in the sports store on Christmas. While riding my motor-bike combination in Middlesex one day in 1966, I was hit by a car turning right too soon across my path, my right knee denting his wing in the process. I was in great pain, unable to get off my combination, while the driver got out of his car and complained about the damage my knee had done to his front wing! The knee didn't heal as quickly as it should have; I was about to leave the R.A.F. at the end of my twelve-year engagement, so I was promptly sent for a course of intensive physiotherapy, at the nearest R.A.F. M.R.U. (Medical Rehabilitation Unit), Chessington. Who should my chief physiotherapist be but that sergeant who loaned me a hammer at the Christmas Island sports store. He chatted with me for quite a while, without letting me slacken off one bit with my painful exercises. Life is full of little surprises.

ON REFLECTION

On reflection, I'm wondering how to reconcile all those enjoyable, even hilarious moments on the island and on the way, with those sobering, sometimes frightening events and their long-term after-effects – that were the backdrop to the whole Grapple series; and personally, on the final leg of my return to U.K., so nearly the end of me. I can appreciate that the hilarities were more fleeting and personal, while the larger, more frightening events were wider in scale. Both, with hindsight are themselves merely frozen moments in time, at their own timescales, one more anecdotal than the other, but both merging into the era of the late fifties. These two disparities do, I think, complement each-other, as life is a kaleidoscope of the exciting and the mundane. Our daily routine fits more or less comfortably in the voids between those marvellous, exciting but fleeting moments in our lives – of dangers faced, of holiday highlights, of music that lifts the soul with pure emotion. These are the moments to savour and remember – rich spices sprinkled into our daily diet of prosaic experience. It is only when we reflect with our own personal memories and thoughts on the larger events, that we relate and hopefully reconcile those contrasting elements with our whole life outlook, maybe sometimes without realising it – on autopilot almost – until years after the event, with time or inclination to reflect with more maturity of hindsight.

Self-drive hire car

Those never-to-be-forgotten experiences were just that; those kinds of gems are retained more keenly; although they may dim with the passage of time, given the right trigger they may be readily recalled and relished – especially if shared. There must be many experiences I went through on the island that I all but completely forgot, but when, for instance, sparked off by meeting others who shared these same events and tasted again afresh, then for each enthusiastic acquaintance there will be separate memories otherwise lost or overlooked until the response kicks in. This has happened to me much more than once, not only for Christmas Island, reminding me of the old adage: "two heads are better than one".

Pete Harrison's 21st party

I found that my memories of these events had dimmed very little with the years, even before sharing them recently with others after such a long time – firstly, with the three firm friends made on the island and kept in contact with over the years – Allan Smith, Dennis King and Paddy Kyle. Secondly with newly formed friends of the B.N.T.V.A. (British Nuclear Test Veterans Association) at our occasional West Yorkshire Branch meetings in Leeds, led by the indomitable cause-fighter, Wally Holdsworth, an early-days nuclear merchant seaman. These all led to a renewed, stronger compulsion to get it all "off my chest" and written down, with the added need to re-publicise the plight of so many of my fellow nuclear guinea-pigs that successive governments have swept under the carpet and preferred to pretend didn't exist. Since joining the B.N.T.V.A., my own perspectives have been further modified and sharpened on the question of contamination and its longer-term after-effects on those who, like me, were present at those nuclear tests. It would seem that many of these victims were present at the earlier, less sanitised, controlled and informed nuclear test stages in Australia, Maralinga and others, when, as I have said, closer to the action, on board ship and when less was known about radiation hazards. But victims I believe they certainly were and remain, especially those who were closer to ground zero.

It has been a most pleasurable experience to talk with fellow veterans about events on Christmas and Australia, even the less pleasant ones, because, as well as their intrinsic interest, they are only one part of the much larger whole of our total nuclear tests experience, which, when added to all the others, built up a store of memories that add essential quality and quantity to the life adventure. Most of this will inevitably be tinged with sadness, as old friends die or suffer chronic illness, but life still goes on.

I need stomach powder!

Memories of those many happy, hilarious, exciting, humorous Christmas experiences, and downright dangerous times, are nowadays tinged with what I would call the darker side of the tests – physical and psychological. I occasionally catch myself pondering the health hazards of those events sixty years ago, although I have to admit that personally, the only after-effects I'm tempted to blame on Christmas Island is a poor short-term memory, which I'm sure I didn't have before. In 1984, my fifteen-year-old daughter nearly lost her life with leukaemia; although she recovered fully, there remains a niggle in the back of my mind of the strong possibility that these events were connected, although all medical specialists we had spoken with at the time assured us that this could not be proved.

Relaxing on the island

Can it be merely co-incidence that, in the years since the tests, the only directly attributable disease linked with our likely contamination situation at the time is leukaemia? My daughter survived, and despite whole-body irradiation that the specialists said destroyed her ovaries twenty years ago, was safely delivered of a beautiful baby boy in January 2003 (although she had no idea she was pregnant until halfway through; also a six-week-premature birth). So – what should my feelings be about my island stay and its health ramifications? Should I wonder how life would have turned out had I not been there, or should I be a cynic, chew the fat on the possibility that my daughter would not otherwise have had leukaemia: how dare such a thing be allowed to happen; who was responsible, and what should be done to show my outrage at her suffering during the prolonged, uncomfortable treatment, especially the nauseous chemotherapy, and whole-body irradiation? Or should I simply be thankful that things turned out the way they did – to forgive and forget – live and let live? I think I prefer the less painful latter course, but at the same time, deep in my sub-conscious, the question will not go away, occasionally re-surfaces and will not leave me entirely at peace.

Fairy Tern, almost tame.

My wife had three miscarriages between 1961 and our first successful live birth in late 1965. Was each one a warning, I wonder: nature's way of disposing of a faulty foetus? We shall never know but will often ponder. Further, this was another condition that was quite a common outcome of the post-nuclear experience.

For us, leukaemia and miscarriages remain incompletely- answered questions, as do all other denials and all other families of all servicemen who have suffered, directly or indirectly, from the after-effects of one debilitating illness or another, cancerous or otherwise. The B.N.T.V.A.s only request is "All we seek is justice". This begs the question: will we ever achieve this, or will successive governments and their scientific advisors and lawyers simply procrastinate and hopefully wait for the problem to go away, when all nuclear veterans have joined the great mushroom cloud in the sky? And yet this is not the end of the matter: adverse conditions have manifested themselves in second and subsequent generations. Why should the imposed sins of the fathers really be visited upon their children?

While on the island, our local occasional newsletter Mid-Pacific News – Grapple Souvenir Edition – of November 1957, contained much open-ended snippets of "officialese", some of which I quote here, with my own comments/questions in brackets; these extracts could still form the basis for discussion today, and have not been taken out of context:

"Radiation hazards…major political issue" (from opposition or party in power at the time?)

"Clarity clouded by ignorance and bias" (whose – ours or theirs?)

"H-bomb radiation levels took a sharp upward rise…of no dangerous significance." (To anyone at all? How do you know so soon afterwards? What a contradiction in terms!)

"High air bursts avoid fall-out……except for a very low level of induced radioactivity near the target area; none at all on the island" (many questions here: how accurate were the altitude-level instruments for the burst? Reports of their malfunction, to almost ground burst level have been made; evidence for and medical results of high-level radioactivity are many; how accurate was "none at all on the island" when so few dosimeters were issued or even available, and how much of the island was monitored? Further, ground zero was only 2.5 km from the south-east tip of the island.)

"Our knowledge renders radiation hazards on this island, of no real significance to anyone except sniffing Canberra crews." (Is this a severe case of over-confidence based on incomplete knowledge of this issue – less on experience and more on misplaced optimism or political expediency?)

"Cannot produce any possible permanent physical injury". (Try telling this to the hundreds (thousands?) of veterans invalided out of the Service and those who still suffer from chronic physical and psychological conditions).

I include these for what they are worth, as they are all directly related to various official departmental descriptions of the Grapple series and were part of an unclassified local island "newspaper". They were only too relevant at the time, of course, and I admit it's all very well quoting in the light of fifty years hindsight and long-past political and international strategic arms policy reversals, but to repeat, they were very relevant to those who served there at the time and who returned with other than a clean bill of health – short or long term.

So, what are the long-term implications? No-one in authority knows or wants to acknowledge, or to venture opinions, let alone take any responsibility for these health problems that can be, I firmly believe, associated with early nuclear test fallout, despite all the official denials. Could this simply and conveniently be labelled a "grey area"? Only with a poor sense of responsibility, I suggest.

Gone native!

I add as a postscript another related aspect of the situation, that obtained then – the stated opinion of the island's Chief Medical Officer at the time -

experienced enough to know what he was talking about. He expressed the view that he could not guarantee the physical or mental well-being of any Serviceman on the island for more than six months. This for me spoke reams for itself, and gave me, if I needed it, a further indication of how potentially hazardous life could be (and was) out there. A salutary opinion I later came to appreciate.

There remain so many unanswered questions in the whole nuclear issue since Grapple and the rest of the nuclear arms race, which begs the question, will they ever by fully resolved or answered at all? How clean was a "clean" bomb, whatever its size and power? How and where detonated? How much can we blame subsequent illnesses on fall-out in its various forms of contamination? Would my daughter have had leukaemia if I hadn't been to Christmas Island? What would have constituted "adequate" protection closer to the bomb? Do we take as gospel the medics' and scientists' answers, opinions, denials and disclaimers made at the time and on many occasions since? What led our prime minister in late 1955 to react to the report of a committee considering the genetic effects of nuclear radiation: "A pity, but we cannot help it"? Although admittedly early days in Britain's post-war nuclear arms testing programme, why could we not learn from Nagasaki and Hiroshima in 1945?

Sunrise Christmas Island

Making sense, or trying to make sense of such a complex, emotive and personal issue would seem to tax the reasoning powers almost to the limit. How do you make a case for and hope to sum up all the many threads of argument for or against this broad, arguably lost, even irrelevant cause that surfaced over fifty years ago? Are the arguments, relevant then, still valid today? To summarise, was it all worth it? Looking around at friends we know, or have lost since that time, convinces me that this cause is still worth pursuing; justice is a basic premise always worth fighting for by those who perceive its merits.

Diamond Head from Punchbowl Hill

Ken McGinley, invalided out of the Army after service in Christmas Island, with a series of chronic debilitating conditions that would not go away (or be fully explained), received so many letters from similarly affected nuclear test veterans – both Service and civilian – as a result of publicity for his own cause, that he formed the B.N.T.V.A. (British Nuclear Test Veterans Association) in 1983, in order to devote himself to fight their corner on their behalf. These hundreds of letters, from veterans, widows and their children, detailed a variety of mysterious, often crippling conditions that could not be explained by the consultants, specialists and family doctors, who examined and treated them – largely unsuccessfully. However, they clearly had their origins most likely at the various nuclear test sites that began in the early fifties, when bombs were "dirtier" and closer, and little was known about the harmful effects of irradiation. At that time, urgency for testing outweighed the need to properly and thoroughly research and assess the safety aspects of proximity to those harmful radiation sources, as was tacitly admitted at a much later stage.

His monumental efforts and research on behalf of his B.N.T.V.A. members gradually resulted in the discovery of contemporary papers that came to light in places such as the Public Records Office at Kew, when previously secret documents were de-classified under the thirty-year rule, conveniently at the time hidden away under contemporary "need-to-know" security. For instance, a study for the B.N.T.V.A.(N.E.) by Danuta O'Neill, S.R.N., S.C.M. entitled "A Very Clean Bomb" of July 1992, Appendix D, gives the distance from land (i.e., the S.E. corner of the island) as 2.5 km (1 ½ miles) for the Grapple X and Y (the largest) megaton detonations. The island is about 25 miles long and most of us were positioned about three quarters of the way towards the N.W. of the island, which gives a maximum distance of about fifteen miles from ground zero, and for many, much less. How near can you get? (Her sources included an I.P.P.N.W. (International Physicians for the Prevention of Nuclear War) Report and a Ministry of Defence document).

and this is what it looks like.

Christmas Island

I suspect that unless you have been personally involved in this contentious issue, few may be unduly bothered one way or the other; after all, this has been a minority issue, meaning that those relatively few concerned are fighting both apathy and political inertia. Is it worth continuing the fight, to ask only for justice or do we just keep hoping that, like the Dickens character, "something will turn up."?

Those of us who survive are mostly in our eighties at least – almost an average lifespan if you don't consider the nuclear tests' long-term health implications. Are we the fortunate ones, to apparently have escaped relatively unscathed, or do we remain aware that future generations may also become affected in some way, as have many already, but unable to prove how it happened or will happen at some time?

Mushroom Cloud – official photograph

At the annual conference of the Leukemia Research at York in April 2008, I asked Dr. David Grant, Scientific Director, for his reaction to my fears of the long-term aftereffects of radiation exposure and the presence of possible genetic abnormalities, for instance in my family. I also asked him about future generations in the light of events so far, and of the chances of any future compensation claims. He reminded me sympathetically that ultimately it all boils down to "burden of proof. Government, Military, and Scientific lawyers will not consider any compensation issues or admissions of responsibility without proof that any condition was the direct result of exposure at the time. This will become increasingly difficult to achieve, even with the recent advances and achievements of our understanding of DNA and the human genome. These unravel what they can tell us about ourselves – our past, present, and possibly our future. Consequently, is it over-optimistic or naïve to expect such an outcome to any of the claims being made by the BNTVA on behalf of its dwindling number of surviving members" (Dr. David Grant, Scientific Director of Leukaemia Research, personal communication).

Kirimati aerial view

And what of the government of the day – are they still procrastinating? After the New Zealand study found, in 2007, that veterans' chromosome alteration could be attributable to radiation, particularly in Operation Grapple, our government still denied this! They have always taken the stance that their legal liability to pay compensation is "only if proved"; also, their "defence of limitation" means they can insist that claims must be made within three years of "injury": (the commonest of these are cancers, skin defects, fertility problems, reduced life expectancy and birth defects to name but a few). The Isle of Man in February 2008, followed other Commonwealth countries' example by paying out compensation to its nuclear test veterans (O.K., there weren't many), so would there be a similar move by our politicians? Well, government funding has recently (February 2008) been agreed, in principle only, for an independent study of test veterans' children and grandchildren (a glimmer of hope in the long term?), but with strict conditions to confirm decisions be credible by scrutinising scientists: they still don't' give things away willingly, do they? But hopefully, it's a start in the right direction.

To their credit, the Sunday Mirror has spearheaded a regular, well-investigated campaign, since October 2000, in support of nuclear test veterans' compensation claims. We need all the support we can get.

CONCLUSION

Those nuclear veterans whose memories are unhappy, may simply want to forget about their life out there, if they are allowed to. That's understandable. I look back and think, did all those things really happen to me in less than one year, fifty years ago? Admittedly I was luckier than some in the variety of my experiences then. I have photographs and slides to remind me (and basic good health), but these are only helpful snapshots of what I did in frozen moments in time out there. My memories add to these, filling in some of the gaps; writing about them has since brought more of them back into clearer focus.

Further, from yet another viewpoint, I feel somehow also better off for those experiences – in a life which includes travel to a diversity of places and environments that continue in semi-retirement; interaction with a true mix of fellow beings, of which stands alone in its wealth of unforgettable events – memories with a vengeance!

Once I had progressed so far with my island story, I knew my summing-up would prove to be the most difficult to present, set down and argue clearly and coherently – the subject so emotive, clouded with personal feelings, fears and opinions, riddled with complexities and blurred with time. I have tried to state things both as they were and as I think they should be, but it must remain a personal view, inevitably biased, but how could it have been otherwise?

On the way to the lagoon

GLOSSARY

AVM = Air Vice Marshall

BFPO = British Forces Post Office

Blighty = Britain

Blues = RAF Blue Uniform

BMH = British Military Hospital

BNVTA = British Nuclear Test Veterans Association

Brass monkey weather = very cold

Civvies = Civilian clothing

CO = Commanding Officer

Cooler = prison

Erk = Low-ranking serviceman

Grapple (X, Y, Z) = Operation codename for Christmas Island thermo-nuclear tests 1957-1958

H bomb = Hydrogen bomb (more powerful version of Atom bomb)

KD = Khaki drill (tan coloured overseas RAF uniform)

Limeys = British

LOA = Local overseas allowance (extra pay for overseas postings to reflect local cost of living expenses)

LPs = Long-playing gramophone records

MATS = Military Air Transport Service (US)

MOD = Ministry of Defence

MRU = Medical Rehabilitation Unit

MT = Mechanical transport

NAAFI = Navy, Army, Air Force Institutes (base shop on all service units)

OGs = Olive greens (overseas Army uniform)

Perks = Incidental benefits attached to a particular job/situation (abbreviation for perquisite)

Pie-dog = Local mongrel dog

PTI = Physical Training Instructor

PWR – Preliminary Warning Roll (for overseas service)

PX = Post-Exchange (American equivalent of NAAFI shops)

RAAF = Royal Australian Air Force

SHQ = Station Headquarters

SNCO = Senior Non-commissioned Officer (Sergeant, Flight Sergeant, Warrant Officer)

SPAL = South Pacific Airlines

SROs = Station Routine Orders

SWO = Station Warrant Officer

Tannoy = Public address system

USAF = United States Air Force

WVS = Women's Voluntary Service

YMCA = Young Men's Christian Association

Zoot suits = Overall white 'uniform' issues for Grapple Y & Z as some measure of protection against flash and heat from larger nuclear detonations

Printed in Great Britain
by Amazon